SECOND EDITION

SENTENCE-
COMBINING
WORKBOOK

Pam Altman

San Francisco State University

Mari Caro

San Francisco State University

Lisa Metge-Egan

Leslie Roberts

WADSWORTH
CENGAGE Learning

Australia • Brazil • Canada • Mexico • Singapore • Spain • United Kingdom • United States

WADSWORTH
CENGAGE Learning™

Sentence-Combining Workbook, Second Edition
Altman/Caro/Metge-Egan/Roberts

Publisher: Michael Rosenberg

Acquisitions Editor: Stephen Dalphin

Development Editor: Cheryl Forman

Managing Marketing Manager: Mandee Eckersley

Senior Marketing Assistant: Dawn Giovanniello

Associate Marketing Communications Manager: Patrick Rooney

Production Coordinator: Jennifer Kostka

Senior Art Director: Bruce Bond

Print Buyer: Betsy Donaghey

Compositor and Production Service: Integra

Cover Designer: Brenda Duke

Cover Photo: © www.comstock.com/ Royalty Free

For product information and technology assistance, contact us at
Cengage Learning Academic Resource Center, 1-800-354-9706

For permission to use material from this text or product, submit all requests online at **www.cengage.com/permissions** Further permissions questions can be emailed to **permissionrequest@cengage.com**

Library of Congress Control Number: 2005938487
ISBN 13: 978-1-4130-1977-3
ISBN 10: 1-4130-1977-3

Wadsworth
25 Thomson Place
Boston MA 02210
USA

Printed in the United States of America
4 5 6 7 8 9 12 11 10 09 08

Contents

Unit Thirteen Modifying Sentences with Verbal Phrases 175

Unit Fourteen Final Review Exercises 183

Preface

To the Student

Most writers, whether experienced or inexperienced, sometimes feel that they just can't get their good ideas down on paper, that something gets lost when they try to express themselves in written words. This book aims to help you become more aware of, and able to use, a variety of ways to express your ideas in the writing that you do for college courses, in your personal lives, and in your future careers.

Throughout this book, you will practice using a variety of sentence combining and expanding techniques so that you will be able to communicate your ideas in fluent, concise, and clear sentence structures. You will find that each unit in this book focuses on a specific sentence-level technique and that each sentence-combining exercise within the units is a story. To make the best use of this book, you should write out all of the solutions to the exercises, read them out loud to make sure your solutions sound right, and finally, proofread them to make sure that you haven't made any errors. And most important, you should use the techniques you practice in the exercises when you write the essays you are working on in your writing course.

If you devote your time and energy to the work of this book, paying close attention with your classmates to the way language works, letting your teacher know whenever you have questions, and applying what you learn to your essay writing, you'll see great improvement in your writing and find that you really can get your good ideas down on paper.

To the Teacher

This book represents a commitment to sentence combining as the most efficient and productive approach to sentence-level skill-building in the basic writing classroom. Units in this book have also been used at levels other than basic writing—in English as a Second Language composition, freshman composition, and remedial writing classes for students of all ages, including foreign graduate students.

George Hillocks, in his meta-analysis of composition research, reports that—

> " . . . extensive reviews of the research are unanimous in concluding that sentence combining 'has been proven again and again to be an effective means of fostering growth in syntactic maturity' (Kerek, Daiker, and Morenberg 1980, p. 1067). Stotsky (1975) even suggests that it 'may facilitate cognitive growth as well' (p. 59), and John Mellon (1979) states that 'the time for action has arrived.' Sentence combining produces no negative effects, and works better than most of the activities in current composition teaching. . . . I don't know of any component in our arsenal of literacy-teaching methods that is better supported empirically than sentence combining. . . . The best advice I can give teachers today, relative to sentence combining, is—Do it!" (p. 35). (<u>Research on Written Composition</u>, 143).

Some studies have also found that basic writers particularly gain from sentence combining—a positive approach that emphasizes the enjoyment of skill-building rather than error avoidance and that builds students' confidence as they see real results in their writing.

But sentence combining cannot be an end in itself; we see the work of this book as the skills-building component of a college composition course in which students analyze information and ideas, making inferences and establishing logical relationships for a purpose.

This book has been used in the basic writing classes at San Francisco State University for several years. Originally written in 1989 and distributed for use at San Francisco State University, it has since undergone many revisions at the suggestions of the editors at Wadsworth Cengage Learning, SFSU composition instructors, Bay Area community college instructors, and students in the basic writing classes themselves, both native speakers of English and bilingual students. The principal author has taught at least four basic writing courses every year since 1985.

Notes on the Second Edition

Continuing our efforts to provide students with opportunities to gain fluency, variety, and cohesion in their writing, we have made several changes to the original text for the second edition. Based on the classroom needs expressed by current users of the first edition, we have added a new unit—Unit Seven: Showing Logical Relationships Using Transition Words. Throughout the text, we have added new exercises, revised and updated others, and clarified explanations and directions.

How to Use This Book

This book is divided into two main sections: sentence joining and sentence modifying, both of which are organized to provide students with practice combining sets of sentences to produce more specific, concise, and fluent sentences. Throughout this book, the emphasis is on <u>doing</u>, rather than analyzing the grammatical structures under practice. Thus, we have avoided extensive explanations about parts of speech or rhetorical purpose.

If you do not feel that your particular class needs a unit, you should adjust the book to fit the needs of your class by skipping a unit or modifying it. But you should consider carefully the review units, which make use of previously-practiced techniques.

We recommend that students spend two 30-minute sessions each week on sentence combining. Most units have the same format: an introduction to the technique to be practiced, an exercise to be done in class, and a follow-up homework exercise. We suggest that the instructor introduce the technique before turning to the book. We also suggest doing the first exercise collaboratively—having students recite their answers to the first two or three sentence sets and then work in pairs on the remaining sets. One student in each pair should write their answer on the board, and once all students have finished and the entire exercise is on the board, the authors should read their answers aloud as the class focuses on each one. This class work gives the instructor the chance to praise success, offer help, and reiterate the essential messages about form and meaning, and it promotes students' attentiveness to language use. Board work also sometimes turns up usage problems, which should always be addressed after the sentence combining has been evaluated. Students should be encouraged to ask questions or to suggest alternatives. To deal with homework exercises, the instructor can ask students to compare their homework with another student's to see if they disagreed. Exercises should be collected and graded. The students should write out all of their answers if the exercises are to have any effect on their writing, and most important, the instructor should always relate the technique under practice to the students' current writing assignment.

Units One and Two are introductory units; Unit One reviews the basic sentence, giving as little in the way of grammar terminology as possible, and serves as background to Unit Two. Unit Two introduces sentence focus, which is both an approach to expressing complex ideas and an editing technique. Composition instructors are of mixed opinions about teaching focus at the basic writing level; some believe that it should be reserved for higher level courses while others believe that basic writers will overcome sentence focus problems just with writing practice and helpful feedback. We know that some basic writers, inexperienced with academic discourse, attempt what they believe to be academic writing by overusing abstract sentence subjects and passive verbs, an approach that for some writers is just a developmental stage. But we believe that teaching sentence focus is helpful for basic writers, some of whom produce sentences that are so misconstructed that the writers themselves don't know why they wrote them—or what they meant to say. Anyone who has taught basic writing must have been at one time or another dismayed by seemingly unclassifiable problems at the sentence level (customarily labeled in the essay margins as "awkward" or "predication error," labels that do nothing to help the basic writer). We believe that teaching sentence focus is a reliable way to approach these problems without burdening students with useless grammar lessons or vague error correction. With genuine writing practice and sentence combining practice, most students will overcome these problems, but the sentence focus guidelines give them a nudge. However, if you are uncommitted to the sentence focus approach, you can skip to Unit Three.

The Review Sections throughout the book are cued exercises (exercises that signal the technique to be used), and should be self-explanatory. The Review Section at the end of the book contains exercises that are not cued but have been carefully written and assessed to allow students to create sentences using the techniques they have practiced in the book.

Semester after semester, in their course evaluations, students write that sentence combining helped them grow as writers and that they had fun doing it. That's what we hope for—that sentence combining will be both enjoyable and purposeful for both students and instructors.

Acknowledgments

For help with the second edition, we are grateful to acquisitions editor Steve Dalphin and development editor Cheryl Forman for their advice and guidance, and to production project manager Jennifer Kostka.

We also want to express our gratitude to the reviewers of this book for their careful evaluation of the text and their many thoughtful suggestions.

REVIEWERS OF THE SECOND EDITION

Patricia Johnson, *Broward Community College*
Deirdre Rowley, *Imperial Valley College*
Brian Strang, *San Francisco State University*
Karen Wong, *Skyline College*

REVIEWERS OF THE FIRST EDITION

Michael Guista, *Allan Hancock College*
Jeffrey Mitchell, *Los Medanos College*
Susan Reiger, *Porterville College*
Karen Wong, *Skyline College*
Susan Zimmerman, *City College of San Francisco*

And thanks, of course, to the thousands of writing students who have devoted their time and energy to the work of this book and rewarded us with the growth all writing teachers hope to see.

Unit One

The Basic Sentence

Throughout this book, you will be combining sentences to practice ways to show logical relationships or to modify, or describe, words in sentences. This practice will help you to express your ideas in clear, concise, and varied sentences when you write college-level essays. But first it helps to know what makes a sentence a sentence. Look at the following groups of words; which do you think are complete sentences?

(a) Teenagers work.
(b) Many teenagers work after school.
(c) Many teenagers work after school to earn spending money.

If you thought that all three are sentences, you are correct, because all three contain a subject-verb unit—a subject and verb working together. Sentence (a) has a verb, the word *work*; it's a verb because it can change form to show the time or tense of an action. So we can say:

Teenagers worked.
Teenagers will work.

Sentence (a) also has a subject, *teenagers*, a word that does the action in the verb. Because sentence (a) has a subject-verb unit, *teenagers work*, it is a complete sentence. Sentences (b) and (c) are also complete sentences; they have the same subject-verb unit as sentence (a) in addition to sentence modifiers that tell more about the subject and verb.

Take a look at the following groups of words; which do you think are complete sentences?

(a) They are.
(b) They are students.
(c) They are students hoping to succeed in college.

Again, all three are complete sentences because they each contain a subject-verb unit—*they are*. But in these sentences, the verb doesn't name an action; the verb is a form of *be*. The common forms of *be* are *am, is, are, was, were, has been, have been,* and *will be*.

To write well, you don't need to know how to identify all of the parts of speech. But if you know how verbs and subjects work together in sentences, you'll find the upcoming work in this book easier, which in turn should help you grow as a writer as you work on focusing, joining, and developing your sentences. In some of the later units, you'll see references to "subjects," "verbs," and "verb forms," so you will benefit in a practical way from the overview of subjects and verbs in this unit.

Recognizing Verbs

You probably know the common definition of verbs—*words that show action or existence*—but that definition is not always helpful when you need to find the subject-verb unit that makes a group of words a sentence. The most reliable way to identify subject-verb units in sentences is to find the verb first and then the subject. To locate the verbs in sentences, you must find the action words or forms of *be* that you can change the tense (time) of.

Exercise One On the Campaign Trail

From each pair of sentences below, you can create one sentence by joining the verbs (with *and* or *or*) and eliminating any repeated words.

EXAMPLE: The presidential candidate travels around the United States.
The presidential candidate makes public appearances.

SOLUTION: The presidential candidate travels around the United States and makes public appearances.

1.   The presidential candidate speaks.
The presidential candidate makes promises.

2.   Some of the people cheer.
Some of the people clap.

3.   Others in the crowd groan.
Others in the crowd hiss.

4.   Secret Service agents watch the candidate.
Secret Service agents worry about the crowd.

5.   The candidate finishes her speech.
The candidate runs to her limo.

Exercise Two   The Last Campaign Trail

Now go back to the sentences in Exercise One and rewrite your combined sentences to show that the actions happened in a *past* election campaign. (You can begin the sentences with *last year*.) Then underline the words you changed to show past time, or tense.

EXAMPLE: The presidential candidate travels around the world and makes public appearances.

SOLUTION: (Last year) The presidential candidate <u>traveled</u> around the world and <u>made</u> public appearances.

1.

2.

3.

4.

5.

The words you changed and underlined are verbs—words that show the time, or tense, of an action, or a form of *be*, in a sentence.

Finding verbs can sometimes be difficult because we often use <u>verb forms</u> as other parts of speech. For example, one form of the word *swim* can be used as a verb, but with an *-ing* ending, it can also be used as a noun (a word naming a person, place, or thing) or an adjective (a word describing a noun).

Alicia swims a mile every lunch hour.   (*swims* = verb)

Swimming is Alicia's favorite way to relax.   (*swimming* = noun)

Alicia would like nothing better than to
have her own swimming pool.   (*swimming* = adjective)

The noun *swimming* and the adjective *swimming* do not change to show the time, or tense, of the sentence. If Alicia decided to give up swimming and start meditating for relaxation, we might write:

Swimming was Alicia's favorite way to relax.

The verb *is* changes to *was* to show past time, but the word *swimming* doesn't change because it isn't acting as a verb here. An *-ing* word can only be part of a verb if it follows a form of the verb *be*:

In her dreams, Alicia <u>is swimming</u> in her own pool.

Exercise Three   Take Me Out to the Ball Game

In each sentence, change each main verb to past time, or tense. Underline the verb; then put in parentheses any verb forms that *don't* change to show time.

EXAMPLE: Listening to the Giants game <u>relaxes</u> me.

SOLUTION: (Listening) to the Giants game <u>relaxed</u> me yesterday.

1.   I listen to the Giants games on the radio.

2.   The announcer bores me by reading so many baseball statistics.

3.   His boring voice puts me to sleep.

4.   I follow the accomplishments of my favorite players.

5.   Barry Bonds is very good at hitting home runs.

6.   I often dream of eating hot dogs and peanuts while I listen to the games.

7.   But going to the ballpark costs more money than listening to the radio.

Using a Dictionary to Choose the Correct Verb Form

To change verb tense, we change the form of the verb, which simply means we add something on the end of the base form (*walk* becomes *walked* to show past tense) or change its spelling (*bring* becomes *brought* to show past tense).

You can find the correct forms of verbs in a dictionary. Look up the base form. Often you know the base form (the form you use with *to—to walk, to sing, to swim*).

If you don't know the base form, you can find it by looking up any form other than the base form. For instance, if you look up the word *sank* in the dictionary, it will direct you to the *to* form of the verb—*sink.*

Once you find the base form, dictionaries list the other verb forms in the same order:

1. **base form**	2. **past**	3. **past participle** (follows *has* or *have*)	4. **present participle** (follows a *be* form)
walk	walked	walked	walking
create	created	created	creating

Like many languages, English has regular and irregular verbs. Regular verbs like *walk* and *create* all show the tense, or time, the same way; for instance, we add an *-ed* or a *-d* to the end of regular verbs to indicate past tense. If a verb is regular, the past and past participle forms are the same, so the dictionary will only list the base and the past forms. To make the past participle forms (forms after *have* or *had*) or the present participle forms (*-ing* forms), you just add the *-ed* or *-ing* ending to the base form.

Verbs that don't follow this predictable pattern are called irregular verbs.

1. **base form**	2. **past**	3. **past participle**	4. **present participle**
be	was/were	been	being
eat	ate	eaten	eating
meet	met	met	meeting

Many of our verbs are irregular, and you may not know all of the past and past participle forms. Sometimes the past and past participle forms of irregular verbs are the same, but sometimes they are not. Any time you aren't sure what a verb's past or past participle form is, you must look it up in a dictionary.

Exercise Four   Write/Wrote/Written

To review some commonly confused irregular verbs, use a dictionary to find the past tense and the past participle forms of the base form verbs listed below.

Base	Past Tense	Past Participle
1. begin		
2. choose		
3. draw		
4. grow		
5. hold		
6. lose		
7. rise		
8. spend		
9. tear		
10. wear		

Exercise Five   Getting a Record

In the following sentences, you are given the past tense of verbs. Change each sentence from past tense to past perfect (with *have* or *has*) by putting the correct past participle in each blank space.

1.   Mark and his friends drove to the record store.

     Mark and his friends have _____ to the record store many times.

2.   They got into an accident on the freeway.

     They have _____ into accidents on the freeway before.

3.   The police led them to the station to file a report.

     The police have _____ many drivers there.

4.   Now Mark has a bad driving record.

     He has _____ a bad driving record since he was 16.

Exercise Six The Onion Cure

Choose the correct past tense or past participle verb form for the verbs given in their base forms. Those in parentheses should be put in past tense form; those in brackets should be put in the past participle form after *have* or *has*.

Not many people _____ of an unpopular but infallible cold remedy that
                              [hear]

my friend Fred recently _____ me about. Fred _____ a large,
                                (tell)   (eat)

raw onion and _____ that it _____ the best cold remedy he
                    (swear)   (be)

_____. He _____ into it like an apple, and though it
      (know)   (bite)

_____ his eyes water, he _____ the potency of the onion
      (make)   (think)

_____ all the germs in his body. Many times I _____ to try this
      (kill)   [want]

magic onion cure, but I _____ afraid to take the first bite.
                              [be]

Recognizing Subjects

Once you have located the verbs in sentences, it's easier to find the subjects—the words that tell who or what does the action or the form of *be* in the verbs.

To locate verbs and subjects, follow this two-step process:

1. Use the time test to find the verb; change the sentence to another time.

    Alicia swims a mile every lunch hour.
    (last year)   Alicia <u>swam</u> a mile every lunch hour.

    To show the change in time, or tense, we changed *swims* to *swam*, so *swims* is the verb.

2. Once you have found the verb, you can locate the subject of the verb by asking yourself:

    Who or what _____?
    verb

    Who or what <u>swims</u> a mile every lunch hour?
    verb

    The answer is *Alicia*, so *Alicia* is the subject of the verb *swims*.

Our example sentence has one subject-verb unit—*Alicia swims*. Often though, verbs can have more than one subject:

<u>Alicia</u> and <u>Tieu</u> <u>swim</u> a mile every lunch hour.

Or subjects can have more than one verb:

<u>Alicia</u> <u>swims</u> a mile and <u>lifts</u> weights every lunch hour.

Or sentences can have more than one subject-verb unit:

<u>Alicia</u> <u>swims</u> a mile every lunch hour, but then her <u>boss</u> <u>treats</u> her to a cheese steak for lunch.

Be sure to look at the whole sentence when you follow the two-step process for finding verbs and subjects so that you are sure to locate all of the subject-verb units.

Exercise Seven   Mind Your Manners

The following groups of words are not complete sentences because they don't have subjects—words that work together with verbs. In the blanks provided, supply a subject to complete each sentence. (It helps to skim the whole story first.)

    EXAMPLE: _____ have terrible manners.

    SOLUTION: <u>Many people</u> have terrible manners.

1. On the freeway, _____ make you tense by tailgating or blasting their horns.

2. In department stores, _____ follow you around, suspecting you of shoplifting.

3. _____ crowd behind you in line for the ATM, trying to see your bank balance.

4. On the bus, _____ won't give up their seats for elderly people or students carrying heavy backpacks.

5. In a concert hall, _____ wear intense cologne spiked with gardenias, vanilla, and cloves.

6. And sometimes in a theater, _____ loudly analyze the plot all through the movie.

7. In restaurants, _____ throw tantrums over fifteen-minute waits for their checks.

8. At baseball games, _____ jump up in front of you right in the middle of a double play.

9. Of all these rude people, _____ bug me the most.

10. _____ should take a course on etiquette.

Exercise Eight   Get a Job

In this exercise, follow the two steps for identifying verbs and their subjects. Underline the verbs once and the subjects twice. Reminder: an *-ing* word can only be part of a verb if it follows a form of the verb *be*, e.g. *am working* and *was thinking*.

EXAMPLE: Most people work in conventional occupations, like accounting, teaching, or retail sales.

SOLUTION:

Step 1: To find the verb, change the time, or tense, of the sentence. To change the time, we have to change *work* to *worked*, so *work* is the verb.

Step 2: To find the subject, ask yourself "Who or what <u>works</u>?" The answer is *people*, so *people* is the subject.   verb

(*5 years ago*) Most <u><u>people</u></u> <u>worked</u> in conventional occupations, like accounting, teaching, or retail sales.

1. Some people have more interesting careers.

2. They become Guillotine Operators, White-Kid Buffers, or Liquid Runners.

3. A Guillotine Operator cuts pencils, not necks.

4. A White-Kid Buffer operates a leather buffer machine, not white kids.

5. A Liquid Runner in a candy factory regulates the flow of syrup.

6. Some people become Gizzard-Skin Removers in a poultry plant.

7. A close friend working as a Bosom Presser irons blouses in a laundry.

8. Her husband, a Top Screw, is the boss of a bunch of cowpunchers.

9. Working in one of these occupations teaches young people about life in the real world.

10. But after reading about these jobs, most people want to get a college degree.

Exercise Nine   Miracle Food

In this exercise, follow the two steps for identifying verbs and their subjects. Underline the verbs once and the subjects twice. Reminder: An *-ing* word can only be part of a verb if it follows a form of the verb *be*, e.g., *is eating* and *has been waiting*.

EXAMPLE: Some food protects people from heart disease.

SOLUTION:

Step 1: To find the verb, change the time, or tense, of the sentence. To change the time, we change *protects* to *protected*, so *protects* is the verb.

Step 2: To find the subject, ask yourself, "Who or what <u>protects</u>?" The answer is *food*, so *food* is the subject.   verb

(10 years ago) Some <u><u>food</u></u> <u>protected</u> people from heart disease.

1. Some health-conscious people eat a handful of almonds a day to lower bad cholesterol.

2. Four servings of fish a week decrease the risk of heart disease.

3. Tuna, salmon and sardines are full of omega-3s.

4. Omega-3s can lower cholesterol and blood pressure.

5. But too much fish raises the level of mercury in the blood, depending on the source of the fish.

6. Eating one clove of garlic a day usually reduces total cholesterol levels, decreasing the risk of heart disease.

7. But after eating garlic, some people worry about offending their friends.

8. The antioxidants in fruits and vegetables can stop cellular damage leading to heart disease.

9. Berries, melons, leafy greens, carrots and broccoli are all full of antioxidants as well as fiber.

10. According to one study, dark chocolate can lower blood pressure, yet the subjects ate only one small chocolate bar each day.

Unit Two

Sentence Focus

At times we read something that doesn't make sense to us, or we write something our-selves, thinking "That's not what I meant to say" or "This doesn't sound right." Chances are that the writing isn't clearly focused on the subject or topic. Your readers will more easily understand your ideas if you focus them clearly, and it's really not so hard to do. Often clear focus in writing depends on clearly-focused sentence subjects.

Read the following paragraph aloud:

Professor Seed suffered through a disastrous first day as a college professor. (a) The way in which he set his alarm clock was wrong, (b) so the early bus was missed and campus wasn't reached until 30 minutes after his first class began. (c) Then the classroom couldn't be found. (d) Help was given by many students, (e) but still the wrong classroom was appeared at by him. (f) Finally the realization came that his wallet was lost, (g) so bus fare had to be borrowed. (h) At home that night, he was told by his wife that the reason he had a bad day was because the wrong foot was started off on.

This paragraph begins with a topic sentence, a sentence that tells the main idea of the paragraph. The topic sentence makes it clear that the subject of the paragraph will be Professor Seed, specifically his first day as a college professor. Yet the focus of the rest of the paragraph isn't clear because *Professor Seed*, the subject of the paragraph and the gram-matical subject of the first sentence, never again appears as a sentence subject.

This paragraph, then, is unfocused; it's hard to figure out *who did what*. By focusing your sentences clearly, you can make sure that your reader understands who performs the action or form of *be* in the verb.

In this unit, you will work on applying guidelines for writing focused sentences, which in turn will help you to keep larger pieces of writing focused.

Here are the two basic guidelines:

- When you begin to write, ask yourself "What subject am I writing about?" The subject/topic of your writing will often be the sentence subject.

- Ask yourself "Who (or what) does what?" The answer should be the sentence subject.

Exercise One Hard Ball

Each of the following sentences begins well, but the parts in parentheses aren't focused clearly. In the blanks provided, rewrite the parts in parentheses so that you keep the focus on the personal, human subject. Ask yourself "who does what?" The answer should be the sentence subject.

EXAMPLE: The employees of Do Nuttin' Bakery often play co-ed softball games, and _____.
(usually a good time is had by everyone)

SOLUTION: The employees of Do Nuttin' Bakery often play co-ed softball games, and <u>usually everyone has a good time</u>.

1. But two teams gathered at Rough Diamond Park on a Sunday afternoon, and _____
(trouble

_____.
was gotten into by everyone)

2. The pitcher, Mary, hit the batter, Tina, with a wild pitch, and _____
(the ball was thrown

_____.
back at Mary by Tina)

3. Tina's teammates charged from the dugout, and _____
(home plate was surrounded by

_____.
Mary's teammates)

4. Tina's team claimed that Mary hit Tina on purpose, but _____
(it was argued by Mary's team

_____.
that a new pitch was just being tried out by Mary)

5.   Finally, Mary demonstrated her new pitch, so _____
                                                                   (it could be seen by everyone why

_____ .
control of the ball was lost by Mary)

6.   Mary pitched an impressive curve ball, but _____
                                                                   (the ball wasn't pitched over home

_____ .
plate by her)

Exercise Two Exam Stress

Sigmund, a college student, is taking an exam in his psychology class, and one of his short-essay questions reads:

What are some of the causes of problems between parents and teenagers?

Immediately Sigmund writes down some points he wants to include in his answer:

1. Rules and expectations aren't made clear.
2. Resentment occurs when chores aren't done.
3. Blame is placed on teenagers for anything that goes wrong in the home.
4. The way in which parents discipline is by yelling too much.
5. The complaint is that teenagers aren't listened to.
6. There isn't the recognition that parents are human beings too.
7. Enough respect isn't shown to parents.

Then Sigmund begins to write his answer:

"The causes of problems between parents and teenagers are . . ."

but he gets stuck before he even begins to show what he knows. Why? He has begun by focusing his first sentence on the subject *causes*, an abstract word, and the verb *are*. It looks like he is going to name <u>all</u> of the causes of problems in one sentence.

Help Sigmund by writing a more clearly-focused beginning sentence. Ask yourself "Who does what?" and make your answer the subject of the sentence.

Write your beginning sentence here:

_____

_____

Now go back and improve the focus of six of the seven sentences in Sigmund's notes. Ask yourself "Who does what?" in each sentence, and make your answer the sentence subject. Write your clearly-focused sentences in the spaces provided. Sigmund's original sentences appear in parentheses below the spaces.

EXAMPLE 1:   (Rules and expectations aren't made clear.)

SOLUTION: <u>Parents don't make their rules and expectations clear.</u>

2. _____
   (Resentment occurs when chores aren't done.)

3. _____
   (Blame is placed on teenagers for anything that goes wrong in the home.)

4. _____
   (The way in which parents discipline is by yelling too much.)

5. _____
   (The complaint is that teenagers aren't listened to.)

6. _____
   (There isn't the recognition by teenagers that parents are human beings too.)

7. _____
   (Enough respect isn't shown to parents.)

Now write three well-focused sentences in which you state what you think are the causes of conflict between teenagers and parents:

1. _____
   _____

2. _____
   _____

3. _____
   _____

Exercise Three   Who's to Blame?

Applying what you know about focusing sentences, now go back to the paragraph about Professor Seed and clarify the focus of the sentences in the paragraph. The original, unfocused sentences are given in parentheses. Ask yourself "Who does what?" and make your answer the sentence subject.

EXAMPLE (a): _____
(The way in which he set his alarm clock was incorrect.)

SOLUTION: He incorrectly set his alarm clock.

b. _____
(so the early bus was missed and campus wasn't reached until 30 minutes after his first class began.)

c. _____
(Then the classroom couldn't be found.)

d. _____
(Help was given by many students,)

e. _____
(but still the wrong class was appeared at by him.)

f. _____
(Finally the realization came that his wallet was lost,)

g. _____
(so bus fare had to be borrowed.)

h. _____
(At home that night, his wife was told that the reason he had a bad day was because the wrong foot was started off on.)

Unit Three

Joining Sentences with Coordinators

When your sentences are clearly focused, you'll find it much easier to join sentences that are logically related. In this unit, you will practice using the seven coordinators. The easiest way to remember them is to remember the word FANBOYS, which is an acronym, a word made up of the first letters of the names of the seven coordinators. In the example sentences below, notice the logical relationships that the coordinators express:

Coordinators		Logical Relationships
FOR:	Mary enjoys math, <u>for</u> it is challenging.	effect/cause
AND:	Thuy has won several trophies, <u>and</u> she is an honor student.	addition
NOR:	Judy doesn't work, <u>nor</u> does she want a job.	addition of negatives
BUT:	Nabil is pretty good at gymnastics, <u>but</u> he prefers swimming.	contrast
OR:	Jaime needs a vacation, <u>or</u> he'll go crazy.	alternative
YET:	Irma doesn't earn much, <u>yet</u> she spends money like a millionaire.	contrast
SO:	The coach praised the team excessively, <u>so</u> the players stopped believing him.	cause/effect

PUNCTUATION: When coordinators join sentences, commas come before the coordinators, following this pattern: *sentence + comma + coordinator + sentence*.

The coordinators are important because:

1.   We can use them to join sentences, which helps eliminate choppiness in our writing.

2.   Unlike other joining words, they can also show logical relationships between two separate sentences; we can begin sentences with coordinators.

Siu Fong practiced gymnastics every day. <u>So</u> she eventually excelled at it.

3.   Most importantly, the coordinators help to express logical relationships between sentences.

Exercise One   Old House

Join the following sets of sentences, using <u>coordinators</u>. The logical relationships are given in brackets.

EXAMPLE: Most people want to own their own home.
            They can't afford one.   *[contrast]*

SOLUTION: Most people want to own their own home, <u>but</u> they can't afford one.

1. Sid and Sal found an old, inexpensive house they could afford.
    They bought it.   *[cause/effect]*

2. They wanted a newer house.
    New houses were too costly.   *[contrast]*

3. Sid and Sal applied for a loan to fix up the dilapidated building.
    The lender approved it.   *[addition]*

4. They replaced the old toilet in the upstairs bathroom.
    The bathtub fell through the rotted floor into the kitchen below. *[contrast]*

5. They were not pleased to find a hornet's nest in the attic.
    They were not happy to find termites in the foundation.   *[addition of negatives]*

6. The house was in danger of collapsing any day.
   The termites had devoured most of the foundation.   *[effect/cause]*

7. Sid and Sal decided they should jack up the house
   to replace the foundation.
   Their house would be a "goner."   *[alternative]*

8. The construction workers had to work on the foundation.
   They lifted the house gently with hydraulic jacks.   *[cause/effect]*

9. The crew completed the foundation.
   The roof caved in.   *[contrast]*

10. Sid and Sal now live in the backyard.
    It's a lot safer than living in their house.   *[effect/cause]*

Exercise Two   Car Shopping

Join the following sentences, again using the <u>coordinators</u>; this time you will choose the coordinators that best show the logical relationships.

> EXAMPLE: Maria decided to buy a new car.
> She didn't know much about cars.

> SOLUTION: Maria decided to buy a new car, <u>but</u> (or <u>yet</u>)
> she didn't know much about cars.

1. She wanted to be a well-informed shopper.
   She began to do research.

2. She bought a stack of popular auto magazines.
   She even found government statistics on car crash tests.

3. She didn't consider gas-guzzling SUVs.
   She needed to save on gas.

4. She was attracted to sport cars.
   The insurance rates on such beauties were outrageous.

5. The most affordable car for Maria was the Zippy Company's compact sedan.
   The car's crash test performance was rated "Extremely Poor."

6.   An expensive, imported station wagon was rated favorably on the crash tests.
     It provided anti-lock brakes and a heavy steel protective body.

7.   Maria needed to test-drive several cars.
     She would not know if they were comfortable enough.

8.   The dealer for Ripoff Company did not treat Maria courteously.
     The overpriced Ripoff Cars did not impress her.

9.   The dealer selling the comfortable, safe, and economical Rightstuff car treated
     Maria with respect.
     She left the dealership in a brand new Rightstuff car.

Unit Four

Joining Sentences with Subordinators

Subordinators are sentence joining words that, like the coordinators, help us show a variety of relationships between ideas. Here are the subordinators we use most often:

Subordinator	Logical Relationship	Example
although, though even though while, whereas	contrast	<u>Although</u> I am a senior, I have 40 more units to take.
because, since	effect/cause	School is taking longer <u>because</u> I have to work.
if	condition	I can go to the movies <u>if</u> I finish my homework.
unless	condition	I cannot go to the movies <u>unless</u> I finish my homework. (if I don't finish)
before, after when, whenever until, as soon as	time	After I finish my homework, <u>I'll</u> go to the movies.

When we put a subordinator in front of a sentence, we change the sentence from an independent clause to a dependent (or subordinate) clause. A dependent clause cannot be a sentence by itself, so we have to join it to an independent clause:

Because she purchased her ticket in advance,   *(dependent clause)*
she got a discount fare.   *(independent clause)*

She got a discount fare   *(independent clause)*
because she purchased her ticket in advance.   *(dependent clause)*

Here is the rule to remember when using the subordinators to join two logically related ideas:

The dependent clause can come first or second in the sentence, but the two logically related ideas must appear in the same sentence.

She bought a ticket in advance.   *(sentence)*
Because she bought a ticket in advance.   *(fragment, not a sentence)*
Because she bought a ticket in advance, she got a discount fare.   *(sentence)*

PUNCTUATION: When the subordinate clause comes first in a sentence, it is followed by a comma, following this pattern: *subordinate clause + comma + independent clause.*

39

Exercise One   Familiar Pests

Combine the following pairs of sentences using <u>subordinators</u>. Make the underlined sentence into the subordinate, or dependent, clause; the logical relationship is given in brackets.

EXAMPLE: <u>Some rodents and birds prey on cockroaches.</u>
Humans are their biggest foes.   *[contrast]*

SOLUTION: <u>Although some rodents and birds prey on cockroaches</u>, humans are their biggest foes.

1. Cockroaches are a health menace to humans.
    <u>They carry viruses and bacteria that cause diseases from</u>
    <u>hepatitis to salmonella</u>.   *[effect/cause]*

2. <u>Humans try to defeat the cockroaches.</u>
    Cockroaches are very successful at surviving.   *[contrast]*

3. <u>Cockroaches are smaller than the humans who chase them.</u>
    They have extremely fast responses and sensitive receptors.   *[contrast]*

4. <u>There is no food.</u>
    Cockroaches subsist on glue, paper, and soap.   *[condition]*

5. <u>They can't find glue, paper, or soap.</u>
    They can draw on body stores for three months.   *[condition]*

6. <u>Cockroaches are really desperate</u>.
    They will turn into cannibals.   *[condition]*

7. Female Surinam cockroaches produce generation after generation
    of identical females.
    <u>They are able to clone themselves</u>.   *[effect/cause]*

8. <u>Cockroaches must have their antennae intact</u>.
    They function well even with their eyes painted over.   *[contrast]*

9. Some scientists believe roaches would survive nuclear war.
    <u>Roaches can tolerate much more radiation than humans</u>.   *[effect/cause]*

10. Scientists have found that cockroaches dehydrate and die.
    <u>They are deprived of their protective waterproof coating</u>. *[condition]*

11. <u>You want to keep cockroaches as pets</u>.
    You should find a way to destroy their waterproof coating.   *[condition]*

Exercise Two   Stay on the Trail

In the following exercise, decide first how the ideas are logically related; then, choose a <u>subordinator</u> that shows the relationship and use it to join the two sentences.

> EXAMPLE: Yoshi was not much of a hiker.
>   He went hiking with his co-worker Jose.

> SOLUTION: <u>Although</u> Yoshi was not much of a hiker, he went hiking with his co-worker Jose.

1.   Jose suggested they go to a State Park in warm Sonoma County.
     It was cold and foggy in San Francisco.

2.   They got to the park.
     They purchased a map of all the trails.

3.   Yoshi chose a rather short trail.
     Jose chose a longer, more challenging trail.

4.   Yoshi agreed to go on the longer trail.
     Jose promised to buy him dinner.

5.   They started out on the trail.
     They left the trail and walked through some tall grass.

6.   Yoshi felt an alarming pain in his arm.
     He suggested they stop and rest for a moment.

7.   Yoshi took off his shirt.
     He found a tick embedded in his arm.

8.   Both Yoshi and Jose knew ticks carry a disease.
     They read *Newsweek* and watched "Nightline."

9.   Ticks, including a few in Sonoma County, carry Lyme Disease.
     Yoshi was not worried.

10. He removed the tick right away.
     He will be less likely to contract the disease.

Joining Words That Show Logical Relationships

Relationship	Coordinators	Subordinators
Addition	and nor	
Cause/Effect	so	
Effect/Cause	for	because since, as
Contrast	but yet	although even though though while whereas
Concession		although even though though while whereas
Alternative	or	
Condition		if whether unless
Time		after, before since, until while, when whenever as soon as

Coordinators can (1) join sentences or (2) introduce complete sentences.

(1)   Lucy has a new computer, <u>but</u> she doesn't know how to use it.
(2)   Lucy has a new computer. <u>But</u> she doesn't know how to use it.

Subordinators can (1) join sentences or (2) introduce sentences if the clauses they are attached to are followed by commas and then by independent clauses.

(1)   Kevin likes his job <u>because</u> he makes a lot of money.
(2)   <u>Because</u> he makes a lot of money, Kevin likes his job.

In the following review exercise, you will use coordinators and subordinators to join sentences and show logical relationships. In some sets, you are asked to join first with a coordinator and then with a subordinator. (Refer to the chart on page 45 for help.)

EXAMPLE: Many people can't seem to live without chocolate.
Scientists wonder if chocolate is addictive.

SOLUTION 1:   Many people can't seem to live without chocolate, <u>so</u> scientists wonder if chocolate is addictive.   *(coordinator)*

SOLUTION 2:   Scientists wonder if chocolate is addictive, <u>for</u> many people can't seem to live without it.   *(coordinator)*

SOLUTION 3:   <u>Because</u> many people can't seem to live without chocolate, scientists wonder if it is addictive.   *(subordinator)*

1.   There are many delicious kinds of chocolate.
Milk chocolate is the most popular kind in the United States.

   a.   Use a coordinator:

   _____

   _____

   b.   Use a subordinator:

   _____

   _____

2.   The average American consumes ten pounds of chocolate every year.
This number is increasing.

   a.   Use a coordinator:

   _____

   _____

3.   Some of us get hooked on chocolate.
The chemicals in chocolate can help us feel good.

   a.   Use a coordinator:

   _____

   _____

   b.   Use a subordinator:

   _____

   _____

4. Pyrazines in chocolate attract humans.
   Pyrazines smell good.

   a. Use a coordinator:

   _____

   _____

   b. Use a subordinator:

   _____

   _____

5. The chemical phenylethylamine appeals to chocolate lovers.
   It gets people out of sad moods.

   a. Use a coordinator:

   _____

   _____

   b. Use a subordinator:

   _____

   _____

6. People consume carbohydrates, a component of chocolate.
   Their moods improve and they feel more alert.

   a. Use a subordinator:

   _____

   _____

7. We can eat chocolate to get all the benefits.
   We may gain weight.

   a. Use a coordinator:

   _____

   _____

   b. Use a subordinator:

   _____

   _____

8. You feel you are addicted to chocolate.
    You have two choices.

    a. Use a subordinator:

    _____

    _____

9. You can quit eating chocolate altogether.
    You can try to eat less.

    a. Use a coordinator:

    _____

    _____

10. Most people won't give up their chocolate habit.
    They can't imagine a life without chocolate.

    a. Use a coordinator:

    _____

    _____

    b. Use a subordinator:

    _____

    _____

Unit Five

Joining Sentences to Show Comparison and Contrast

In your college courses, and in your personal lives and professional careers as well, you will frequently compare and contrast people, things, or ideas. Employers often must compare and contrast two or more job applicants, college students may compare and contrast two historical periods, and people often compare and contrast two products they are considering buying, or two people they know. By joining ideas or information with coordinators and subordinators, you can clearly show similarities and differences to your reader.

For example, because two college freshmen, George and Paul, are twin brothers, we expect them to be similar, but they are actually different in some ways. Here are random lists of information we have gathered about them:

George	**Paul**
is tall and slim	has brown eyes and brown hair
likes to read science fiction	is tall and slim
runs three miles daily	still hasn't found a major
has brown eyes and brown hair	likes to read poetry
works as a cartographer's assistant 15 hours per week	hates to exercise
is an engineering major	works 20 hours per week as an usher in a theater

The above information about the twins is not listed in any organized way. So after we gather information about two subjects (in this case, the twins), the next step toward comparing and contrasting them is to organize the lists according to related points, here the twins' physical descriptions, interests, jobs, and college majors:

George	**Paul**
has brown hair and brown eyes	has brown hair and brown eyes
is tall and slim	is tall and slim
likes to read science fiction	likes to read poetry
runs three miles daily	hates to exercise
works as a cartographer's assistant 15 hours per week	works 20 hours per week as an usher in a theater
is an engineering major	still hasn't found a major

We can now express the similarities and differences between the twins in sentences using the coordinators and subordinators that you reviewed in Units Three and Four.

Exercise One   George and Paul

The sentences below express the similarities and differences between the twins, George and Paul. In each sentence, circle the joining word(s) that show comparison or contrast and then list the words you've circled below.

1.   Both George and Paul have brown eyes and brown hair.

2.   George and Paul both are tall and slim.

3.   George likes to read science fiction, but Paul likes to read poetry.

4.   George runs three miles daily, yet Paul hates to exercise.

5.   While George works as a cartographer's assistant 15 hours per week, Paul works 20 hours per week as an usher in a theater.

6.   Although George is an engineering major, Paul still hasn't found a major.

Comparison Words   **Contrast Words**

In addition to showing the similarities and differences between people, we often compare and contrast behavior, cultures, theories, points of view on an issue, the positive and negative features of something, or the past with the present. The exercises in this unit give you practice in using coordinators and subordinators to compare and contrast activities, cultures, and a past and present condition. The following chart summarizes the joining words that show the logical relationships of comparison and contrast.

Summary of Comparison and Contrast Joining Words

	Comparison	Contrast
COORDINATORS	and	but, yet
SUBORDINATORS		although
		even though
		though
		while
		whereas

Coordinators can join sentences and begin sentences. When they join sentences, place a comma before the coordinator.

Kim likes heavy metal, but Tom prefers classical music.
Kim likes heavy metal. But Tom prefers classical music.

Subordinators join dependent clauses to sentences. When the dependent clause comes first, place a comma after it; if the dependent clause follows the independent clause, don't use a comma.

While Kim likes prime rib, Tom prefers rice and vegetables.
Kim likes prime rib while Tom prefers rice and vegetables.

Exercise Two   Getting in Shape

Carl wants to begin a regular exercise program, but he can't decide between running and walking. To make a rational choice, he lists what he knows about each activity:

Running

improves cardiovascular endurance
burns 800 to 1,000 calories per hour
can be done in an urban or rural area
can cause shinsplints and muscle strain
requires no special equipment

Walking

can be done in an urban or rural area
is relatively injury-free
requires no special equipment
improves circulation and posture
burns 300 calories per hour

Step 1:   Organize the two lists according to related points:

Running	**Walking**
1. can be done in an urban or rural area	can be done in an urban or rural area
2.	
3.	
4.	
5.	

Step 2:   Using the coordinators *and*, *but*, and *yet*, and the subordinators *while*, *whereas*, *although*, (or *even though*, and *though*), write five sentences in which you compare and contrast running and walking, using the information you organized in Step 1.

1.

2.

3.

4.

5.

Exercise Three   The Nuer and the Bakhteri

In this exercise, you will compare and contrast two cultures—the Nuer and the Bakhteri. Here are random lists of information about the two cultures:

The Nuer

are pastoral people
divide labor according to sex
occupy a flat, grassy region
use products from cattle for shelter and food
live in the Sudan
raise dairy cattle
women herd the cattle

The Bakhteri

men herd the sheep and goats
live in Southern Iran
are pastoral people
raise sheep and goats
divide labor according to sex
occupy a mountainous area
use products from sheep and goats for
    shelter and food

Step 1:   Complete the following lists by organizing the information according to related points.

	The Nuer	The Bakhteri
1.	are pastoral people	are pastoral people
2.	live in the Sudan	live in Southern Iran
3.		
4.		
5.		
6.		
7.		

Step 2: Write sentences in which you join related similarities and differences using the coordinators and subordinators that show comparison and contrast. Follow the examples below.

1. Both the Nuer and the Bakhteri are pastoral people.

2. The Nuer live in the Sudan while the Bakhteri live in Southern Iran.

   You should create five more sentences from your lists in Step 1. <u>Be sure to use a variety of coordinators and subordinators that show contrast.</u>

3.

4.

5.

6.

7.

Exercise Four   The Netsilik and the Trobriands

Following the two steps you took in Exercises Two and Three, compare and contrast two cultures—the Netsilik and the Trobriands. Organize the lists, then write six sentences using joining words that show comparison and contrast.

The Netsilik

hunt seals and caribou
occupy a cold desert environment
live on the Arctic Coast
migrate seasonally
build houses of snow and ice
value the extended family

The Trobriands

live in villages all year
value the extended family
are horticulturists whose primary crop is yams
occupy warm coral Islands
live on the Trobriand Islands off the coast
    of New Guinea
build wooden houses clustered
    in small villages

Step 1:   Organize the lists.

1.

2.

3.

4.

5.

6.

Step 2:   Combine related points into sentences using coordinators and subordinators. Be sure to use a variety of coordinators and subordinators that show contrast.

1.

2.

3.

4.

5.

6.

Comparing the Present and the Past

While attending her 25-year high school reunion, Jonita saw her old boyfriend Peter, whom she hadn't seen since graduation. She was surprised by the changes in him, and wrote a letter to her best friend describing the changes:

> Peter has changed a great deal in the last 25 years. Although Peter <u>had</u> curly red hair 25 years ago, he now <u>has</u> almost no hair at all. While he once <u>played</u> basketball, now he just <u>watches</u> sports on TV. He <u>hated</u> to read in school, but now he <u>reads</u> all the time. In high school, he <u>wanted</u> to be an engineer, but today he <u>teaches</u> history at a junior college. Most importantly, in high school, he <u>vowed</u> to stay single forever, yet now he <u>is</u> a married man with two children.

When we compare and contrast the past with the present, we have to be careful of verb tenses so that the time is clear for our readers. Notice that Jonita uses the past tense forms of verbs to describe Peter's condition 25 years ago and present tense forms of verbs to describe the way he is now. Watch for <u>time words</u> that indicate which tense should be used:

Time	**Past Tense**	*Time*	**Present Tense**
25 years ago	<u>had</u> curly red hair	*now*	<u>has</u> almost no hair
once	<u>played</u>	*now*	<u>watches</u>
in school	<u>hated</u>	*now*	<u>reads</u>
in high school	<u>wanted</u>	*today*	<u>teaches</u>
once	<u>vowed</u>	*now*	<u>is</u>

Exercise Five   The Middleton Boom

In the following paragraph, fill in each blank with the correct tense of the given verb. Notice that the topic sentence makes it clear that the paragraph will show the differences between Middleton in the past and Middleton now. (It helps to skim the entire passage before filling in the blanks.)

The town of Middleton has changed a great deal in thirty years. Thirty years ago, its

population _____ 3,000, while now it _____ 43,000. Many of the
          be   *be*

current residents now _____ in the insurance business, a business that
                        work

_____ not exist until 1975, when Pay Up Insurance Company _____
    do   *establish*

its headquarters there. Immediately the insurance business _____ unemployed
                                                              attract

workers from all over the state who in turn _____ the need for new services.
                                              create

Before 1975, Middleton _____ no libraries, yet now it _____ three,
                        have   *have*

each adjacent to new high schools, which _____ built within a three-year
                                           be

period from 1979 to 1982. Students graduating from middle school formerly _____
                                                                            go

to high school in a neighboring town, but now they _____ school in their home town.
                                                     attend

Unit Six

Joining Sentences to Show Concession

Read the following short paragraphs and follow the directions below them.

1. Both Hunk and Rabbit are star quarterbacks. They both play for the Middleton Marvels and both have been invaluable players. Hunk is fast and strong, and Rabbit is too.

Circle the joining words and list them here:

2. Both Hunk and Rabbit are star quarterbacks, but they have different strengths. Hunk has had more experience in pro football, but Rabbit is young and learns quickly. Rabbit has a strong arm and executes long passes well, yet Hunk is precise on short and medium-range passes. Rabbit is fast, but Hunk can make quick decisions on the line of scrimmage.

Circle the joining words and list them here:

3. Although Hunk and Rabbit are star quarterbacks, they have different strengths. While Rabbit is young and learns quickly, Hunk has had more experience in pro football. Even though Rabbit has a strong arm and throws long passes well, Hunk is precise on short and medium-range passes. Whereas Rabbit is fast, Hunk can make quick decisions on the line of scrimmage.

Circle the joining words and list them here:

    After reading paragraph 3, do you have the sense that the writer thinks one player is better than the other? Which one? Why?

The Concessive Subordinators

We use the contrast subordinators *although, even though, though, while,* and *whereas* to show contrast. But they do more than just show contrast: they **de-emphasize** the points they are attached to and, at the same time, show **concession**. When we concede a point, we admit that it has value. Concessive subordinators are highly useful in presenting written arguments because they allow us to concede, or admit, that an opposing point has merit and at the same time, to de-emphasize the opposing point's importance to the reader.

    For example, football fans in the town of Middleton disagree about who the starting quarterback on the Middleton Marvels should be—Hunk or Rabbit. The local newspaper has invited readers to submit their opinions in letters to the editor.

A fan in favor of Hunk writes:

> Although Rabbit has a strong arm and executes long passes well, Hunk is precise on short and medium-range passes, so he should be the starting quarterback.

A fan in favor of Rabbit writes:

> Although Hunk is precise on short and medium-range passes, Rabbit has a strong arm and executes long passes well, so he should be the starting quarterback.

Using the same information about the two quarterbacks, both fans have used *although* not only to contrast the two players, but also to concede that the competitor does have good points; at the same time, the writers de-emphasize the competitor's good points. (The fans could also use the subordinators *while* and *whereas*, but *although*, *even though*, and *though* are the strongest concessive subordinators.)

Conceding a point shows that we acknowledge that an issue is complex and that in forming our opinion, we have considered the opposition. People who read an opinion that merely states, "Rabbit has a strong arm and executes long passes well, so he should be the starting quarterback," will wonder, "But what about Hunk's precision on short and medium-range passes?" and will be less likely to value the writer's opinion.

Summary of Contrast and Concession Words

	Contrast	Concession
COORDINATORS	but, yet	
SUBORDINATORS	although even though though while whereas	although even though though while whereas

Choosing Contrast Coordinators or Subordinators

<u>Coordinators</u> give equal emphasis to the ideas they join.

<u>Subordinators</u> de-emphasize the ideas they are attached to.

Practice in Contrast and Concession: Two Neighborhoods

Americans often move to new locations because they are leaving home to go away to school, taking a new job, buying a home to accommodate a growing family, or retiring to a place more hospitable to the elderly. Whatever our reasons for moving, we try to find a neighborhood that will best suit our needs and lifestyles.

In the following exercise, you will be contrasting two neighborhoods in Marina City, or contrasting one neighborhood's advantage with a disadvantage. You will be either joining two sentences to simply show contrast or joining two sentences to show contrast <u>and</u> concession and to emphasize information about one neighborhood.

Remember that the coordinators *but* and *yet* show contrast, giving equal emphasis to the ideas they join, while the subordinators *although, even though, though, while,* and *whereas* show contrast and concession, de-emphasizing the points they are attached to.

Directions for joining are given in italics.

EXAMPLE 1:	Sunny Hills is close to public transportation.
	Sea View is near a beautiful park.

a.   Show contrast; give equal emphasis:

SOLUTION:	Sunny Hills is close to public transportation, <u>but</u> Sea View is near a beautiful park.
EXPLANATION:	To give equal emphasis to the good features of the two neighborhoods, we use the coordinator *but* (or *yet*) to join and contrast the two sentences.

b.   Show concession; emphasize the good point of Sea View:

SOLUTION:	<u>Although</u> Sunny Hills is close to public transportation, Sea View is near a beautiful park.
EXPLANATION:	We emphasize the good feature of Sea View by placing the concessive subordinator *although* before the information about Sunny Hills. We admit that Sunny Hills has a good feature, but we emphasize the good feature of Sea View.

EXAMPLE 2:   Sea View is near a beautiful park.
Sea View is far from the college campus.

a.   Show contrast; give equal emphasis:

SOLUTION: Sea View is near a beautiful park, <u>yet</u> it is far from the college campus.

b.   Show concession; emphasize the distance from campus:

SOLUTION: <u>Even though</u> Sea View is near a beautiful park, it is far from the college campus.

Exercise One   Sunny Hills and Sea View

1.   Sea View is close to a museum.
     Sunny Hills has its own swimming pool and bike paths.

     a.   *Show contrast and give equal emphasis:*

     _____

     _____

     b.   *Show concession and emphasize the advantage of Sea View:*

     _____

     _____

2.   Sunny Hills is close to the college campus.
     Sunny Hills has limited parking.

     a.   *Show concession and emphasize a disadvantage of Sunny Hills:*

     _____

     _____

     b.   *Show concession and emphasize an advantage of Sunny Hills:*

     _____

     _____

3.   Sunny Hills is close to a shopping mall.
     Sea View has many small shops and cafes.

     a.   *Show contrast and give equal emphasis:*

     _____

     _____

     b.   *Show concession and emphasize a good feature of Sea View:*

     _____

     _____

Exercise Two   My Neighborhood

In the following exercise, you will join sentences to show people's points of view about their neighborhoods, using the underlined concessive subordinators *although*, *even though*, *though*, *while*, and *whereas* to concede a point and, at the same time, to de-emphasize it while emphasizing what's important to the resident.

Directions are given in italics; choose the most important information to emphasize by identifying what is most important to the resident named in the directions.

EXAMPLE: Sea View has no nightclubs or dance spots.
Sea View is close to the city's main library.

a.   *Join from the point of view of a college student who loves to party more than study:*

SOLUTION: While Sea View is close to the city's main library, it has no nightclubs or dance spots.

b.   *Join from the point of view of a college student whose first priority is doing research:*

SOLUTION: Although Sea View has no nightclubs or dance spots, it is close to the city's main library.

1.   Sea View has two great cafes.
Sea View is far from campus.

a.   *Join from the point of view of a college student without a car, whose most important concern is having a way to get to school:*

_____

_____

b.   *Join from the point of view of a professor with a car whose day isn't complete unless she has her morning espresso at a local cafe:*

_____

_____

2.   Sunny Hills has several outstanding public schools.
Sunny Hills has an excellent private school.

a.   *Join from the point of view of a parent of two children in public schools:*

_____

_____

b.   *Join from the point of view of a parent of two children in private school:*

_____

_____

3. Sea View has poor public transportation.
    Sea View has many services for senior citizens.

    a.   Join from the point of view of a retired man in his 70s:

    _____

    _____

    b.   Join from the point of view of a woman who rides the bus to work:

    _____

    _____

4. Sea View has great ocean views.
    Sea View is far from the freeway.

    a.   Join from the point of view of a computer specialist who must commute by freeway daily:

    _____

    _____

    b.   Join from the point of view of a person who rarely leaves home:

    _____

    _____

5. Sunny Hills has an outdoor swimming pool and bike paths.
    Sunny Hills has no fitness centers.

    a.   Join from the point of view of a physically active outdoors person:

    _____

    _____

    b.   Join from the point of view of a guy who likes to lift weights in front of an admiring audience:

    _____

    _____

6. Sunny Hills has many neighborhood problems.
    Sunny Hills has active community organizations.

    a.   Join from the point of view of a resident who'd just like peace and quiet:

    _____

    _____

    b.   Join from the point of view of a community activist who loves working for a good cause:

    _____

    _____

Practice in Contrast and Concession: Alternatives to Gasoline

Most vehicles in the United States use only gasoline and diesel, both made from oil. To reduce pollution, transportation costs, and dependence on imported oil, U.S. government regulators, automakers and consumers are considering alternative fuels. Take a look at the chart below, which lists the advantages and disadvantages of different alternative fuels, because it contains information that you will use in sentence combining in Exercises Three and Four.

Contrasting the Fuel Alternatives

	Advantages	Disadvantages
Gasoline	available everywhere	pollutes the environment
	technology in place	unreliable foreign sources
100% Biodiesel	domestically-produced	limited availability
	made from renewable plant and animal sources	expensive sources
Electricity	produces zero emissions	made at polluting power plants
	car batteries re-chargeable at home	long re-charging times
Hydrogen Gas	almost pollution free	costly to produce and distribute
	produced from renewable natural gas resources	difficult to fit large fuel tanks on cars
Compressed Natural Gas	comes from vast domestic gas reserves	difficult to fit large fuel tanks on cars
	clean-burning, non-petroleum	long tank-filling times

In the following exercise, you will join sentences using the coordinators *but* and *yet* to contrast fuels and give equal emphasis, and you will use the subordinators *although*, *even though*, *though*, *while*, and *whereas* not only to contrast fuels, but also to emphasize a point and show <u>concession</u>.

You will see two sentences, followed by directions for joining them, given in italics.

EXAMPLE: Compressed natural gas comes from vast domestic gas reserves.
Biodiesel is made from renewable plant and animal sources.

a. Show contrast; give equal emphasis:

SOLUTION: Compressed natural gas comes from vast domestic gas reserves, <u>but</u> biodiesel is made from renewable plant and animal sources.

EXPLANATION: Here we joined the two sentences with the <u>coordinator</u> *but* (or *yet*) to simply contrast the two fuels and give equal emphasis to their advantages.

b. Show concession; emphasize the advantage of compressed natural gas:

SOLUTION: <u>Although</u> biodiesel is made from renewable plant and animal sources, compressed natural gas comes from vast domestic gas reserves.

EXPLANATION: To emphasize the advantage of compressed natural gas, we placed the concessive subordinator *although* in front of the sentence about biodiesel. Now we have de-emphasized the advantage of biodiesel and emphasized the advantage of compressed natural gas. At the same time, we joined the two sentences, showed contrast, and conceded, or admitted, that biodiesel does have a good quality.

Exercise Three   Alternatives to Gasoline

Join the following sets of sentences, following the directions given in italics. Remember that coordinators and subordinators both show contrast, but the coordinators *but* and *yet* give equal emphasis to the sentences they join, and the subordinators *although*, *even though*, *though*, *while* and *whereas* de-emphasize the ideas they are attached to. Refer to the previous page for examples.

1. Gasoline is available everywhere.
   Electric car batteries are rechargeable at home.

   a. *Show contrast and give equal emphasis:*

   _____

   _____

   b. *Show concession and emphasize the advantage of gasoline:*

   _____

   _____

2. Electricity requires long re-charging times.
   Compressed natural gas requires long tank-filling times.

   Show concession and emphasize the disadvantage of compressed natural gas:

   _____

   _____

3. Electricity produces zero emissions.
   Electricity is made at polluting power plants.

   Show concession and emphasize electricity's good point:

   _____

   _____

4. Biodiesel is made from renewable plant and animal sources.
   These sources are expensive.

   Show concession; emphasize the disadvantage of biodiesel:

   _____

   _____

Exercise Four   Taking a Stand

From the chart on page 75, choose the fuel that you think is best, and state your opinion in a sentence here:

Using information from the chart, complete the following:

1. Write a sentence in which you concede, or admit, an advantage of another fuel while emphasizing an advantage of your fuel:

    _____

    _____

2. Write a sentence in which you concede a disadvantage of your fuel and emphasize a disadvantage of another fuel:

    _____

    _____

3. Write a sentence in which you concede a disadvantage of your fuel and emphasize one of its advantages:

    _____

    _____

4. Consider the pollution that can be generated in a car using your fuel.

    If your fuel pollutes the environment, write a sentence in which you concede the pollution problem while emphasizing an advantage of your fuel.

    _____

    _____

    If your fuel does not pollute the environment, write a sentence in which you concede a disadvantage of your fuel and emphasize the fact that it doesn't pollute:

    _____

    _____

Unit Seven

Showing Logical Relationships with Transition Words

In addition to the two categories of joining words you've studied—coordinators and subordinators—we have another category of words that shows logical relationships between ideas—**transition words**, like *however* and *therefore*. Unlike coordinators and subordinators, <u>transition words do not join sentences</u>.

To see how writers use transition words, you can skim through published writing, looking for transition words. But you'll discover that they are hard to find because writers use them sparingly, mainly to show relationships or make connections between idea units, or sets of ideas, while using coordinators and subordinators more frequently to join sentences.

Using Transition Words Effectively

Here are some examples of transition words used effectively in published writing:

1. *an excerpt about the navigational abilities of birds:*

   Columbus made his first landfall in America by altering course to the southwest when he observed huge flights of land birds heading in that direction, while the discovery of Brazil may also be due to the navigator Pedro Cabral taking advantage of bird flights as natural pilotage. **Thus**, in our long history of exploration and discovery, we have often been glad to use the built-in skills and navigational instincts of animals, themselves also a long way from home.

   Peter Evans, *Ourselves and Other Animals*

2. *a paragraph from a composition textbook:*

   A common image of the United States is the rather convivial melting pot of immigrants. If this country were a melting pot, it would be the case that all who arrived and remained here mixed together easily into a diverse new whole. **However**, a thoughtful examination of the many waves of immigrants, their relationships with one another, and the impact of immigrants on the native population of America shows that the mixing has been anything but easy.

   Judith Stanford, *Now and Then*

3. *an excerpt from a paragraph about friendships between animals:*

   Lucy, a chimpanzee reared by humans, was given a kitten to allay her loneliness. The first time she saw the little cat, her hair stood on end. Barking, she grabbed it, flung it to the ground, hitting out and trying to bite it. Their second encounter was similar, but at their third meeting she was calmer. As she wandered about, the kitten followed her, and after half an hour Lucy picked it up, kissed it and hugged it, marking a complete change of attitude. **Subsequently** she groomed and cradled the kitten, carried it constantly, made nests for it and guarded it from humans.

   Jeffrey Moussaieff Masson and Susan McCarthy
   When Elephants Weep: The Emotional Lives of Animals

4.   *a paragraph from a reference text:*

Weather systems change as they travel over Earth because they contact different surfaces and encounter different weather systems. Their atmospheric components are related, and components change as systems form and dissipate over time. **For example**, a system that forms over a tropical ocean, such as a hurricane, changes rapidly by losing temperature and wind speed as it moves over relatively cold, upper-latitude landmasses.

The National Geographic Society,

The National Geographic Desk Reference

Using Transition Words Correctly

Because transition words <u>do not join</u> two sentences, we have to be aware of the correct ways to use them. We have two choices:

1)   We can join two logically-related sentences with a semi-colon (;) and show the logical relationship with a transition word:

Many parents and educators are concerned about childhood obesity; **therefore**, some public school districts have banned the sale of sodas on school grounds.

The semi-colon joins the two sentences, and the transition word *therefore* shows the logical relationship between them. Generally, we use this pattern when we are showing the logical relationship <u>between two sentences</u>.

2)   We can separate the logically-related sentences with a period, and show the logical relationship with a transition word:

Many parents and educators are concerned about childhood obesity. Besides promoting good exercise habits in children, these adults hope to encourage good nutrition at home and at school. **Therefore**, they want public school districts to ban the sale of high-calorie sodas on school grounds.

The transition word *therefore* shows the logical relationship between the first two sentences and the last sentence. Generally we use this pattern when we are showing the logical relationship <u>between two idea units</u>.

On the following page, you'll see a chart listing the transition words used most often. You can refer to this chart as you complete the exercises in this unit.

Showing Logical Relationships with Transition Words

Logical Relationship	Transition Words
Addition	also, moreover, in addition, furthermore besides
Cause/Effect	therefore thus as a result hence consequently
Comparison	similarly likewise
Contrast	however nevertheless nonetheless on the other hand on the contrary
Alternative	instead, rather on the other hand
Condition	otherwise
Time	then next afterwards subsequently first, second, third . . . finally meanwhile in the meantime
General to Specific	for example for instance
Restatement	in other words

Exercise One   Making Connections

In this exercise, read the entire passage and then decide what transition word would effectively show the logical connection between the idea units. Write the transition word you select in the blank space.

EXAMPLE: Many American public school districts have banned the sale of sodas on school grounds because they are concerned about the growing epidemic of childhood obesity. But some parents and educators claim that a ban on soda sales alone won't be effective because children will still buy sodas, or other beverages or snacks with high-sugar content, off campus. _____, they propose that schools provide students with more opportunities for exercise and more information about nutrition during school hours.

SOLUTION: The last sentence in the above passage expresses an effect of the opinion expressed in the previous sentence, so any transition word showing a cause/effect connection—*therefore, thus, as a result, consequently,* or *hence*—would work. *Instead* is also possible because it shows that the parents' and educators' proposal is an alternative to the school districts' ban on soda sales.

1. Whenever I clean my car, I have to spend a lot of time removing junk that has accumulated beneath the seats and in the trunk before I can vacuum the interior and clean the leather, plastic and metal parts. _____, I wash and dry the exterior and congratulate myself for a job well done.

2. Some students and teachers are concerned about the discussion of controversial issues in the classroom. Some students fear that they will be graded on whether or not they agree with the teacher's viewpoints, or they are afraid to express a minority opinion, or an opinion that isn't politically correct. _____, some teachers are concerned that a student may feel uncomfortable if the classroom discussion turns to a topic that is taboo in a student's culture or religious group. Others worry that the class will go off track and they won't get around to covering the course material.

3. Since I have several siblings and only one television, we often battle about which TV program to watch. Sometimes we take a vote, and the majority gets to enjoy the show of their choice. _____, the losers wait impatiently until the program is over, often interrupting to criticize the show.

4.   Some people oppose stem cell research, if it involves embryonic stem cells that come from fertilized eggs donated by patients in fertility clinics. These opponents believe that fertilized eggs are already human life. _____, scientists can sidestep the controversy surrounding the use of fertilized eggs by creating embryonic stem cells through merging unfertilized eggs with other body cells, such as skin cells.

5.   Once Madeline decided that she needed to lose weight, she began to make a plan because she knew that she wouldn't naturally change her junk-food or couch-potato habits. She knew that group support would help keep her on track. _____, she enrolled in a fitness club and joined Weight Watchers.

Exercise Two   Touring Museums

In the following exercise, you will show logical relationships between sentences using transition words. Decide how the two ideas are logically related; then, choose a transition word to show the logical relationship. Join the two sentences with a semi-colon and the transition word.

> EXAMPLE: After he finishes his college education, Robert hopes to become an art appraiser.
> He's majoring in art history and minoring in business.

> SOLUTION: After he finishes his college education, Robert hopes to become an art appraiser; **therefore**, he's majoring in art history and minoring in business.

1.   Melissa and Robert wanted to escape the foggy San Francisco summer and visit museums. They took a weekend trip to sunny Los Angeles.

2.   After purchasing plane tickets in San Francisco, they flew to the Los Angeles Airport, rented a compact car, and drove to West LA. They checked into a motel and went for a swim.

3.   After swimming for an hour, they decided over lunch to spend one day visiting museums. They wanted to spend one day at the beach and another day at Universal Studios.

4.   Melissa wanted to go to the Museum of Jurassic Technology to study the seed-gathering behavior of mobile home dwellers. Robert wanted to go to the California Heritage Museum to see California pottery.

5. They could have spent the day arguing about where to go.
   They decided to compromise.

6. They went to the Museum of Jurassic Technology in the morning.
   They went to the California Heritage Museum in the afternoon.

7. Melissa learned a lot about the behavior of seed gatherers.
   She learned that they preserve seeds of indigenous plants.

8. Robert discovered many California potters he had never heard of.
   He saw pottery from the Arts and Crafts movement.

9. When they returned to San Francisco, Melissa started planning another trip.
   Robert started visiting the local museums.

10. Since their trip was so successful, next year they're going to the Metropolitan Museum in New York.
    They might go to the Art Institute of Chicago.

Exercise Three   Smooth Traveling

While it's important to know how to use transition words correctly, it's also important to know when to use them effectively to keep our writing fluent. Read the paragraph below out loud, making sure to pause when you come to a period:

> I have always enjoyed traveling. Therefore, I do it as often as I can. For example, every summer I get away, preferably to another country either in South America or in Europe. However, I don't always get a chance to leave this country. My bank account is sometimes low. Furthermore, I am sometimes too busy to take off a month or two to travel. Nevertheless, I usually do everything I can to get away. For example, I will work 55-hour weeks, spend nothing on myself, and go without luxuries such as a car or dining out, just to save enough money for my trips. In addition, I even try to survive on peanut butter sandwiches or baked potatoes to save money for my plane tickets.

What is the problem with this paragraph? What do you hear? _____

Here's the same paragraph, but now without the transition words.

> I have always enjoyed traveling. I do it as often as I can. Every summer I get away, preferably to another country either in South America or in Europe. I don't always get a chance to leave this country. My bank account is sometimes low. I am sometimes too busy to take off a month or two to travel. I usually do everything I can to get away. I work 55-hour weeks, spend nothing on myself, and go without luxuries such as a car or dining out, just to save enough money for my trips. I even try to survive on peanut butter sandwiches or baked potatoes to save money for my plane tickets.

In this exercise, rewrite the above paragraph, using coordinators and subordinators to join logically-related sentences. Is there a place where a transition word would be effective?

If you need more space, you can continue writing on the back of this page.

SUMMARY: Transition words can be effective ways to show logical connections between ideas—to make transitions clear for readers. But it's important to use them effectively and correctly, to make sure that they don't take over your writing. Aim to use transition words to show logical relationships between sets of ideas, and use a variety of coordinators and subordinators to show logical connections between two sentences.

Unit Eight

Joining Parallel Structures

The coordinators *and*, *or*, and *but* can join parts of sentences; the sentence parts are called parallel because they are similar grammatical structures that express similar ideas. The parallel structures in the sentences below are underlined:

<u>Shauna</u> and <u>Lisa</u> watch movies every weekend.
Shauna <u>laughs</u> or <u>cries</u> all during the films.
Lisa eats popcorn <u>constantly</u> but <u>quietly</u>.

In the following exercise, you will be joining sets of sentences like the ones below. (Notice the crossed-out words; when you join parallel structures, you can be more concise because you avoid repeating words.) The joining word *and*, *or*, or *but* is given in brackets to tell you which word to use.

EXAMPLE: Latisha ate a burrito.   *[and]*
~~Latisha ate~~ a taco.

SOLUTION: Latisha ate a <u>burrito</u> and a <u>taco</u>.

EXAMPLE: Rudy started the car.   *[and]*
~~Rudy~~ backed out of the driveway.

SOLUTION: Rudy <u>started</u> the car and <u>backed out</u> of the driveway.

Exercise One The Decision

1. Sonia was planning to move into the dorms.   **[or]**
    Sonia was planning to move into an apartment with a friend.

2. She listed the benefits of each place.   **[and]**
    She listed the drawbacks of each place.

3. The apartment was close to campus.   **[and]**
    The apartment was close to the mall.

4. The dorm fee was more expensive.   **[but]**
    It included room and board.

5. She could have her own room in the apartment.   **[but]**
    She would have to share a dorm room with another student.

6. Sonia knew her friend was studious and responsible.   **[but]**
    Sonia didn't know what her dorm roommate would be like.

7. Sonia discussed her options with her parents.   *[and]*
   Sonia discussed her options with her friends.

8. Her parents thought she should wait a year before moving out.   *[and]*
   Her friends agreed.

9. Sonia chose to reject her parents' advice.   *[and]*
   Sonia chose to reject her friends' advice.

10. She decided to enroll in Clown College.   *[or]*
    She decided to at least join the local circus.

Joining Three or More Parallel Ideas

The coordinators *and*, *or*, and *but* can also join three or more elements in a sentence; all of the elements should have similar grammatical structures.

EXAMPLES: <u>Shauna</u>, <u>her boyfriend</u>, and <u>Lisa</u> watch movies every weekend.

Latisha ate a <u>burrito</u>, a <u>taco</u>, and a <u>banana split</u>.

Rudy <u>started</u> the car, <u>backed out</u> of the driveway, and <u>crashed</u> into the potted plant.

Often a series of parallel structures has descriptive modifiers:

Yesterday I <u>finished</u> my homework,
         <u>took</u> my sister to the dentist,
         <u>cooked</u> dinner,
and   <u>went</u> to bed at midnight.

The important thing is that the parallel parts—the verbs *finished*, *took*, *cooked*, and *went*—all have the same grammatical structure and can follow the sentence subject—*I*.

Exercise Two   The Cosmic Navy

Combine the following sets of sentences to create one sentence that contains a parallel series of two, three, or four parts. The coordinators are given in brackets.

EXAMPLE: Fenwick joined the Cosmic Navy.
His sister Sally joined the Cosmic Navy.   *[and]*
His best friend Morton joined the Cosmic Navy.

SOLUTION: Fenwick, his sister Sally, *and* his best friend Morton joined
the Cosmic Navy.

1. They wanted to travel around the world.
They wanted to learn about different cultures.   *[and]*
They wanted to become independent.

2. Fenwick thought he could become a captain.   *[or]*
Fenwick thought he could become an admiral.

3. Morton wanted to make a lot of money.   *[and]*
Morton wanted to meet a lot of people.

4. Sally wanted experience as a naval engineer.   *[and]*
Sally wanted opportunities to do undersea photography.

5. Sally became an excellent underwater photographer.
Sally was promoted to captain.   *[and]*
Sally began to give orders to Fenwick and Morton.

6. Fenwick soon realized that he would never become an admiral.   *[or]*
   Fenwick realized that he would never become a captain.   *[and]*
   He grew tired of taking orders.

7. Morton met a lot of people.   *[and]*
   Morton made a lot of money.   *[but]*
   He didn't have any place to spend it.

8. Fenwick decided to stage a mutiny.   *[and]*
   Morton decided to stage a mutiny.   *[but]*
   They disagreed over tactics.

9. Fenwick wanted Morton to disguise himself as a dolphin.
   Fenwick wanted Morton to swim alongside the ship.   *[and]*
   Fenwick wanted Morton to distract Sally while he took over the ship.   *[but]*
   Morton wanted to bribe Sally.   *[and]*
   Morton wanted to take command of the ship himself.

10. Sally discovered their plot.   *[and]*
    Sally threatened to give them galley duty.   *[or]*
    She threatened to abandon them at the next port.   *[but]*
    Fenwick promised to pose underwater for her.   *[and]*
    Morton bought everyone a round of drinks.

Exercise Three   You Be the Co-Author

In this exercise, you will create parallel structures matching the underlined words to complete the sentences. Remember to join the parallel structures with *and*, *but*, or *or* before the last item in the list of parallel structures. Try to use all three of the coordinators that join parallel structures.

EXAMPLE: My favorite foods are <u>burritos,</u> _____
_____

SOLUTION: My favorite foods are burritos, <u>pasta, broccoli, peaches and chocolate cake</u>.

1.   To have a happy childhood, children should have a <u>safe home,</u> _____
_____

2.   Once I graduate from college, I'll <u>go</u> to graduate school, _____
_____

3.   People can protect the environment by <u>recycling,</u> _____
_____

4.   I sometimes envy students who are good at <u>statistics,</u> _____
_____

5.   I'd like to travel to <u>Mexico,</u> _____
_____

6.   I wish the U.S. government would <u>provide</u> better health care, _____
_____

7.   My closest friend is <u>reliable,</u> _____
_____

8. Whenever I'm looking for a job, I <u>search</u> the want-ads, _____

   _____

9. I spent the weekend <u>cleaning</u> my kitchen, _____

   _____

10. <u>Watching</u> movies, _____

    _____

    are my favorite things to do.

In the following exercise, you will use <u>coordinators, subordinators, and parallel structures</u> to create one sentence from each set of sentences. The logical relationships, and suggestions for using coordinators or subordinators to express the relationships, are given in brackets. You will have to discover which parts of sentences can be joined with *and*, *or*, or *but* to form parallel structures. Always plan your solution and read your combined sentences aloud.

EXAMPLE: People have long argued about whether genes determine our personalities the most.
People have long argued about whether the environment determines our personalities the most.
[coordinator—contrast] Now many scientists believe that nature and nurture work together.

SOLUTION: People have long argued about whether genes or the environment determines our personalities the most, <u>but</u> now many scientists believe that nature and nurture work together.

1.   Scientists now believe that genes determine only the brain's main circuits of neurons. Scientists now believe that the environment shapes the trillions of connections between neurons.

2.   *[subordinator—time]* Babies are born.
Their brains have trillions of neurons.
[coordinator—contrast] Only some of these neurons are functional.

3.   Some of the neurons have already formed circuits that regulate breathing.
The circuits regulate heartbeat.
The circuits regulate body temperature.
The circuits regulate reflexes.

4. Other neurons have not formed circuits.
    [coordinator—cause] These neurons become functional only when they respond to outside stimuli.

5. *[subordinator—condition or time]* The neurons are stimulated.
    They are integrated into the circuitry of the brain.
    [subordinator or coordinator—cause] They connect to other neurons.

6. *[subordinator—condition]* The neurons are not stimulated.
    The neurons may wither.
    The neurons may die.

7. Childhood experiences stimulate neurons.
    Childhood experiences determine whether a child will be confident.
    Childhood experiences determine whether a child will be fearful.

8. Experiments with rats show new evidence that the neurons can be stimulated with play.
    Experiments are with monkeys.
    Experiments are with human babies.
    The neurons can be stimulated with purposeful training.

9. Scientists have found that music helps develop children's brain circuits.
    [coordinator—cause] Parents should sing songs with their children.
    Parents should play structured, melodic music.
    Parents should give their children music lessons.
    [subordinator—condition] Their children show musical aptitude.
    Their children show musical interest.

102

10. *[subordinator—time]* Children listen to classical music.
    They exercise neurons.
    They strengthen circuits for mathematics.
    [subordinator—cause] The brain circuits for math are close to the circuits for music.

11. Scientists have found that talking to children helps develop children's brain circuits for language.
    [coordinator—effect] Parents should talk to their children a lot.

12. Parents can also influence their children's circuits for emotions.
    [subordinator—condition] The parents recognize their children's emotions.
    The parents return their children's emotions.

13. *[subordinator—condition or time]* A parent approves of his or her child's happiness.
    The child's circuits for happy emotions are reinforced.

14. *[subordinator—condition or time]* A parent disapproves of his or her child's happiness.
    The circuits are confused.
    The circuits will not strengthen.

15. *[subordinator—condition or time]* A parent hugs an upset child.
    The child learns to calm him- or herself down.

16. *[subordinator—condition or time]* A parent yells at an upset child.
The child doesn't learn to calm him- or herself down.
[subordinator or coordinator—cause] The parent's response does not stimulate
the circuits for calming down.

17. But the parent's actions have to be repeated over time.
[subordinator or coordinator—cause] One mistake will not scar a child for life.

18. *[subordinator—cause]* Environmental influences begin very early in life.
People often confuse them with genetic causes.
[coordinator—contrast] Actually, the environmental stimuli are crucial for
development.

Unit Nine

Modifying Nouns with Adjectives

In conversation and in writing, we often use descriptive words to add meaning to nouns—to modify them. Nouns are words that name persons, places, or things. A sentence subject is usually a noun:

The <u>mayor</u> spoke.

But all nouns do not act as sentence subjects; one sentence can have several nouns with different functions in the sentence:

The <u>mayor</u> spoke to the <u>reporters</u> about his <u>plans</u>.

In this unit, you will practice modifying nouns to create concise, detailed sentences; in the following exercises, you will be given both the nouns and the modifiers. You will first see a base sentence with its nouns underlined:

The <u>doctor</u> spoke to the <u>patient</u>.

Then you will see one or more sentences repeating those underlined nouns and providing you with new information to use to modify the nouns in the base sentence. Be sure you find all the new information; one way to do so is to cross out any repeated words and any forms of the verb *be* in the sentences containing modifiers.

EXAMPLE:　The <u>doctor</u> spoke to the <u>patient</u>.
~~The doctor was~~ sympathetic.
~~The patient was~~ overweight.

Then add the adjective modifiers to the basic sentence:

SOLUTION:　The sympathetic doctor spoke to the overweight patient.

<u>In each set of sentences, your goal is to end up with one sentence</u>. Always read your combined sentences aloud to see if they sound correct to you. These exercises will help you write more detailed, professional sentences.

NOTE:　When you add a modifier before a noun, you sometimes have to change the article in the base sentence from *a* to *an* or *an* to *a* because the modifier you add begins with a different letter than the noun does. Use *a* before words beginning with <u>consonant sounds</u>, and *an* before words beginning with <u>vowel sounds</u>.

EXAMPLES:　a dog　　a horse　　a university

an apple　　an hour　　an umbrella

Exercise One   Never Too Young

1. <u>Doctors</u> are concerned about the <u>population</u>.
    The doctors are diligent.
    The population is American.

2. They have warned them to modify their <u>diets</u> for <u>years</u>.
    The diets are daily.
    The years are many.

3. But <u>Americans</u> continue to eat too much <u>food</u>.
    The Americans are stubborn.
    The Americans are busy.
    The food is fatty.
    The food is convenience.

4. <u>Amounts</u> of <u>food</u> can cause <u>levels</u> that, in turn, can cause heart disease.
    The amounts are large.
    The food is high-fat.*
    The levels are high.
    The levels are cholesterol.

---

*Hyphenated adjectives like *high-fat*, *health-conscious*, or *middle-aged* act like one-word modifiers and go <u>before</u> the nouns they modify:

Jack has been following a <u>low-cholesterol</u> diet for years.

5. Of course, not all <u>people</u> are at <u>risk</u>.
    The people are healthy.
    The risk is high.

6. In particular, <u>doctors</u> believe that <u>people</u> who have a <u>history</u> of <u>disease</u> should be
    concerned.
    The doctors are conscientious.
    The people are middle-aged.
    The history is family.
    The disease is coronary.

7. The thing for all <u>people</u> to do is cut down on <u>food</u>.
    The people are health-conscious.
    The food is fatty.
    The food is highly processed.

8. <u>People</u> can start now to protect their health by eating more <u>beef</u>, <u>chicken</u>, and <u>fish</u>,
    <u>fruit</u> and <u>vegetables</u>, and <u>milk</u>.
    The people are younger.
    The beef is lean.
    The chicken is skinless.
    The fish is broiled or baked.
    The fruit and vegetables are fresh.
    The milk is low-fat.

Verb Forms as Adjectives

In the previous exercise, each modifier you added was a single adjective that you placed in front of the noun it modified. But verb forms can also act like adjectives and modify nouns:

The movie <u>is frightening</u> the child.   The child <u>is frightened</u> (by the movie).
→ the *frightening* movie   → the *frightened* child

    The *-ing* forms (present participles) and the *-ed* forms of verbs (past participles) can often modify nouns. Notice that when *frightening* and *frightened* are parts of verbs in sentences, they follow forms of the verb *be: am, is, are, was, were, has been, have been, had been.* But when these *-ing* and *-ed* ending verb forms modify nouns, they are not parts of verbs any longer; that is, they do not show the time, or tense, of sentences. The following are common verb form modifiers:

-ing Form   **-ed Form**

the *interesting* novel   the *interested* reader
the *terrifying* train ride   the *terrified* passengers
the *annoying* salesclerk   the *annoyed* shoppers

    If the verb form modifier is a single word, you can place it <u>before</u> the noun it modifies:

EXAMPLE: The <u>farmer</u> ran from the <u>bull</u>.
               The farmer was *frightened*.
               The bull was *charging*.

SOLUTION: The *frightened* farmer ran from the *charging* bull.

Often though, we modify nouns with modifiers that have more than one word:

-ing Form   **-ed Form**

the man *buying the book*   the book *bought at Green Apple*
the woman *building the bridge*   the bridge *built by the woman*

When the modifier is more than one word, it comes <u>after</u> the word it modifies.

Exercise Two   Double Dutch

In this exercise, the nouns to be modified are underlined. Add the common adjectives and the verb form modifiers before or after the nouns they modify. One-word modifiers should come <u>before</u> the nouns they modify, and modifiers of more than one word should come <u>after</u> the nouns they modify.

EXAMPLE: Many <u>adults</u> remember Double Dutch as a <u>game</u>.
~~The adults are~~ American.
~~The adults are~~ reminiscing about their childhoods.
~~The game was~~ played on their neighborhood streets.

SOLUTION: Many American adults reminiscing about their childhoods remember Double Dutch as a game played on their neighborhood streets.

1. Double Dutch is a <u>sport</u>.
    The sport is demanding.
    The sport is competitive.
    The sport is played by jumpers skipping within two spinning jump ropes.

2. Every year, thousands of <u>teenagers</u> compete to be on <u>teams</u>.
    The teenagers are talented.
    The teenagers are living all over the world.
    The teams are representing their schools and clubs.

3. A <u>form</u> has become popular.
    The form is new.
    The form is called fusion.
    The form is combining rope jumping and dancing.

4. <u>Teams</u> perform <u>routines</u> in <u>competitions</u>.
    The teams are youthful.
    The routines are sophisticated.
    The routines are accompanied by rhymes, rhythm and blues, or rap.
    The competitions are international.

5. The <u>jumpers</u> execute <u>steps</u>.
   The jumpers are agile.
   The steps are including "The Scissor Jump" and "The Caterpillar."

6. Some <u>teams</u> jump to <u>music</u> and <u>rap</u>.
   The teams are award-winning.
   The teams are Japanese.
   The music is traditional.
   The rap is hardcore.

7. The jumpers sense the ropes' <u>beat</u>.
   The beat is set by the rope turners.

8. Double Dutch probably originated with <u>rope-makers</u>.
   The rope-makers were Phoenician, Egyptian and Chinese.
   The rope-makers were spinning rope from hemp.

9. The <u>rope-makers</u> made a <u>game</u> from their <u>work</u>.
   The rope-makers were resourceful.
   The game was leisure-time.
   Their work was demanding.

10. Many people are surprised that this <u>game</u> is called Double Dutch.
    The game is urban.
    The game is practiced primarily by African Americans.

Exercise Three   Hairdos—The Assyrians and Us

In the following exercise, you will continue adding adjectives and verb form modifiers to the base sentences, but this time the nouns to be modified aren't underlined for you. In the sentences containing modifiers, cross out repeated words and forms of the verb *be*—*am, is, are, was,* and *were*.

EXAMPLE: In the ancient world, the Assyrians were the hair stylists.
~~The Assyrians were~~ inhabiting Iraq.
~~The hair stylists were~~ the first.
~~The hair stylists were~~ real.

SOLUTION: In the ancient world, the Assyrians inhabiting Iraq were the first real hair stylists.

1.   The Assyrians cut hair in layers, so a man's head was like a pyramid.
The layers were graduated.
The man was fashionable.
The pyramid was Egyptian.

2.   Hair was arranged in curls and ringlets.
The curls were cascading.
The ringlets were tumbling over the shoulders.

3.   Men grew beards.
The beards were neatly clipped.
The beards were beginning at the jaw.
The beards were layered in ruffles over the chest.

4.   Women also wore beards.
     Women were high-ranking.
     The beards were stylized.
     The beards were fake.
     The beards were designed to make the women appear like powerful men.

5.   Kings, warriors, and noblewomen had their hair curled with a bar.
     Their hair was abundant.
     Their hair was flowing.
     The bar was fire-heated.
     The bar was iron.

6.   Now people have hair styles or heads.
     The people are young.
     The hair styles are sculpted.
     The heads are partially shaven.
     The heads are decorated with letters or designs.

7.   But women don't wear beards.
     The women are modern.
     The beards are designed to give them equal status to men.

© Wadsworth Cengage Learning

Unit Ten

Modifying Nouns with Prepositional Phrases

Prepositional phrases, groups of words beginning with prepositions like *in*, *on*, *near*, *of*, *with*, *about*, *at*, *to*, *for*, and *from*, can also modify nouns. Prepositional phrases have many purposes.

They often tell place:

We bought a house *in the country*.
The keys *on the desk* are mine.
She owns the cafe *near the railroad station*.

But they often give other information as well:

Everyone knows the dangers *of smoking*.
I bought a car *with a sunroof*.
She wrote a novel *about evil politicians*.

In this unit, you will use prepositional phrases to modify nouns. Like other modifiers of more than one word that you studied in Unit Nine, prepositional phrases come <u>after</u> the nouns they modify:

EXAMPLE: The <u>dance club</u> admits <u>everyone</u>.
~~The dance club is~~ for teenagers.
~~Everyone is~~ between 18 and 21.

SOLUTION: The dance club for teenagers admits everyone between 18 and 21.

Just as you did in the exercises on adjective modifiers in the previous unit, try crossing out repeated words and forms of the verb *be* in the sentences containing the prepositional phrases; then, place the prepositional phrases after the nouns they modify in the base sentence.

Exercise One   The Great Outdoors

In this exercise, the nouns you should modify are underlined. Create one sentence from each set of sentences, placing the prepositional phrases after the nouns they modify. As you did in the adjective modifier unit, cross out repeated words and forms of *be* in the sentences containing prepositional phrases.

EXAMPLE: Brian rarely leaves his <u>home</u> for <u>trips</u>.
~~His home is~~ in the city.
~~The trips are~~ in the wild.

SOLUTION: Brian rarely leaves his home in the city for trips in the wild.

1.   A <u>group</u> persuaded my cousin <u>Brian</u> to join them on a camping <u>trip</u>.
The group was of outdoorsmen.
My cousin Brian is from New York.
The trip was to Yosemite National Park.

2.   They rented a <u>car</u>, set out for Yosemite, and got caught in <u>traffic</u>.
The car was with a <u>rack</u>.
The rack was for their camping gear.
The traffic was from San Francisco.

3.   When they finally arrived at midnight, they found a <u>campsite</u>.
The campsite was for backpackers.
The campsite was next to a stream.

4.   His friends hung their <u>bags</u> in a tree, but Brian hid his <u>pack</u> in his tent.
His friends' bags were of food.
Brian's pack was of candy bars and romance novels.

5. Throughout one <u>night</u>, Brian heard strange <u>noises</u> and felt strange <u>lumps</u>.
    One night was of terror.
    The noises were outside the tent.
    The lumps were under his sleeping bag.

6. When they awoke the next day, they discovered they had chosen a <u>campsite</u>.
    The campsite was under a pine tree.
    The campsite was next to a sleeping bear.

7. After cooking <u>breakfast</u>, the <u>group</u> went on a <u>hike</u>.
    The breakfast was of freeze-dried eggs and applesauce.
    The group was of tired campers.
    The campers were in shorts and t-shirts.
    The hike was to the top of a waterfall.

8. The <u>trail</u> was crowded with experienced <u>hikers</u>.
    The trail was beside the waterfall.
    The hikers were in raingear.

9. While his drenched companions hiked ahead, Brian returned to the campsite,
    grabbed his <u>pack</u>, and moved to a <u>motel</u>.
    His pack was of romance novels and candy bars.
    The motel was with a swimming pool and a restaurant.
    The motel was on the outskirts of Yosemite.

10. <u>Anyone</u> prefers a <u>roof</u>, a <u>floor</u>, and a <u>restaurant</u>.
    Anyone is in his right mind.
    A roof is over his head.
    A floor is under his feet.
    A restaurant is within walking distance.

Exercise Two   Global Warming

In this exercise, you will again practice using prepositional phrases to modify the underlined nouns. Plan your solutions by crossing out repeated nouns and forms of the verb *be* in the sentences containing prepositional phrase modifiers.

EXAMPLE: A radical <u>shift</u> is under way and human <u>dependence</u> is at least partly to blame.
~~The shift is~~ in the Earth's climate.
~~The dependence is~~ on fossil fuels.

SOLUTION: A radical shift in the Earth's climate is under way, and human dependence on fossil fuels is at least partly to blame.

1.   <u>Heat</u> enters the atmosphere and warms the <u>surface</u>.
The heat is from the Sun.
The surface is of the Earth.

2.   Carbon-dioxide and other greenhouse gases trap the heat, causing global warming—rising <u>temperatures</u> and rising <u>levels</u>.
The temperatures are in climates.
The climates are throughout the world.
The rising levels are of oceans.

3.   The <u>burning</u> is the main <u>source</u> that produces greenhouses gases.
The burning is of fossil fuels.
The source is of human-caused carbon dioxide.

4.   Currently, <u>emissions</u> are expected to double in the next 100 years unless <u>people</u> take action.
The emissions are of greenhouse gases such as carbon dioxide, methane, and nitrous oxides.
The people are throughout the world.

5. Already there are <u>signs</u>.
    The signs are of far-reaching ecological effects.

6. <u>Glaciers</u>, the Greenland ice cap, and the ice <u>shelves</u> are shrinking.
    The glaciers are in the Swiss Alps.
    The ice shelves are of Antarctica.

7. We are also witnessing the <u>growth</u>.
    The growth is of El Niños.
    The growth is in strength and frequency.

8. Most scientists think that a rapid <u>change</u> will produce more frequent and severe
    droughts and floods, widening <u>epidemics</u>, and greater <u>loss</u>.
    The change is in the Earth's climate.
    The epidemics are of infectious diseases.
    The loss is of biological diversity.

9. Scientists are studying alternate <u>forms</u>, including fuels made from fermented grasses,
    solar <u>panels</u>, and vast <u>networks</u>.
    The forms are of energy.
    The panels are on rooftops.
    The networks are of wind turbines, hydroelectric dams, and big heat exchangers.

10. Fortunately, there is no <u>shortage</u>.
    The shortage is of solar energy, the primary <u>alternative</u>.
    The alternative is to fossil fuels.

In the following review exercises, you will practice using the modifiers from Units Nine and Ten—adjective and verb form modifiers and prepositional phrases. This time the nouns to be modified are not underlined. Continue crossing out repeated words and forms of the verb *be*.

EXAMPLE: Since the 6th century A.D., people have seen a beast.
~~The people are~~ in the Scottish Highlands.
~~The beast is~~ strange.
~~The beast is~~ in a lake.
~~The lake is~~ deep.
~~The lake is~~ dark.
~~The lake is~~ called Loch Ness.

SOLUTION: Since the 6th century A.D., people in the Scottish Highlands have seen a strange beast in a deep, dark lake called Loch Ness.

1.   In the 20th century, scientists have tried to substantiate tales.
The tales are outlandish.
The tales are of the monster.
The monster is now named the Loch Ness Monster, or Nessie.

2.   Witnesses report that the monster is a creature.
The monster is 20-feet long.*
The creature is long-necked.
The creature is full-bodied.
The creature is with eyes.
The eyes are large.
The eyes are oval-shaped.
The eyes are on top of a head.
The head is small.
The head is snakelike.

3.   Many stories come from residents and observers.
The stories are about the monster.
The residents are respected in the community.
The observers are visiting from Europe and abroad.

*When a modifier showing size is placed before a noun, the word denoting size is singular; we say a *20-foot-long monster*, *60-pound girl*, or *20-yard line*.

4. Some of the stories may be legends.
   The stories are told by residents.
   The residents are along Loch Ness' shores.
   The legends are old.
   The legends are passed down from grandparents to children.
   The children are gathered around firesides.

5. Some people believe the tales are plots to attract tourists.
   The plots are created by hotel owners and shopkeepers.
   The tourists are gullible.
   The tourists are hoping to spend money.

6. Tourists can buy models or plaques.
   The models are miniature.
   The models are of the monster.
   The plaques are commemorative.
   The plaques are imprinted with Nessie's picture.

7. Some biologists believe the monster is really an otter, a deer, or a log.
   The otter is large.
   The otter is playing in the water.
   The deer is swimming across the lake.
   The log is half-submerged.
   The log is decaying.

8. Other scientists believe Nessie could be a descendant of reptiles.
    The reptiles were giant.
    The reptiles were ocean-dwelling.
    The reptiles were trapped in lakes.
    The lakes were inland.
    The lakes were cut off from the ocean by glaciers.

9. Particles make the lake difficult to explore.
    The particles are coffee-colored.
    The particles are peat.
    The particles are floating in the water.
    The lake is deep.
    The lake is steep-sided.

10. Teams have investigated Loch Ness with searchlights, radar, cameras, submarines, and equipment.
    The teams are of scientists.
    The radar is underwater.
    The cameras are underwater.
    The submarines are manned.
    The equipment is recording.
    The equipment is packed inside oil drums.
    The oil drums are watertight.

11. In the 1970s, scientists accepted proof.
    The scientists are renowned.
    The scientists are from all over the world.
    The proof is of Nessie's existence.
    The proof is in the form of photographs.
    The photographs are showing features.
    The features are facial.
    The features are of an object.
    The object is living.

12. But scientists still don't know what the object is.
    The object is unidentified.
    The object is swimming.

With each set of sentences, create one sentence, using simple adjectives and verb form adjectives and prepositional phrases to modify nouns. Plan your solution by crossing out repeated nouns and forms of the verb *be* in the sentences containing the modifiers. Be sure to read your sentences out loud after you finish each one.

EXAMPLE: Sutro Baths was a palace.
~~Sutro Baths was~~ at the end.
~~The end is~~ northern.
~~The end is~~ of Ocean Beach.
~~Ocean Beach is~~ in San Francisco.
~~The palace was~~ huge.
~~The palace was~~ of swimming pools.
~~The pools were~~ for the whole family.

SOLUTION: Sutro Baths, at the northern end of Ocean Beach in San Francisco, was a huge palace of swimming pools for the whole family.

1. The swimming pools were the baths in an era.
The swimming pools were completed in 1894.
The baths were the largest.
The baths were enclosed.
The baths were saltwater.
The baths were in the world.
The era was of many pools.
The pools were indoor.
The pools were saltwater.

2. In 1894, more than 20,000 people attended the inauguration.
The people were pleasure-loving.
The inauguration was featuring a concert and races.
The concert was orchestral.
The races were by swimmers.
The swimmers were competitive.

3. Sutro Baths also had a museum, a gallery, and a gymnasium.
    The museum was exhibiting collections.
    The collections were various.
    The collections were in display cases.
    The gallery was of photographs.
    The gymnasium was filled with trapezes and rings.

4. Visitors descended a staircase to pools.
    The staircase was wide.
    The staircase was bordered with trees.
    The trees were palm, pomegranate, and magnolia.
    The pomegranate trees were flowering.
    The magnolia trees were fragrant.
    The pools were glass-enclosed.
    The pools were facing the ocean.

5. Visitors could choose between a plunge and other pools.
    The plunge was large.
    The plunge was L-shaped.
    The plunge was unheated.
    The other pools were of temperatures.
    The temperatures were varied.
    The other pools were including one bath.
    The bath was freshwater.

6. Water came from basins and a spring.
    The water was for the pools.
    The basins were constructed in the cliffs.
    The cliffs were fronting the ocean.
    The spring was ever-flowing.
    The spring was freshwater.

7. Around the pools were tiers and balconies.
    The tiers were of seats.
    The seats were for 5,000 people.
    The balconies were for 15,000 more spectators.
    The spectators were wandering.

8. Each tier had corridors.
    The corridors were decorated with plants, fountains, and creatures.
    The plants were tropical.
    The creatures were stuffed.
    The creatures were in life-like poses.

9. By 1952, Sutro Baths had undergone changes.
    The changes were many.
    The changes were including the additions and the closing.
    The additions were of an ice-skating rink and a beach.
    The beach was interior.
    The beach was tropical.
    The closing was of the pools.
    The pools were deteriorating.

10. But Sutro Baths closed in 1952 and the remains burned to the ground.
    The baths were costly.
    The remains were of the building.

11.   Now San Franciscans swim in pools.
        The pools are crowded.
        The pools are chlorinated.
        The pools are divided into lanes.
        The lanes are for lap swimmers.

Review Exercises 5 and 6 make use of all of the structures you have learned in previous lessons: <u>adjective modifiers, prepositional phrase modifiers, coordinators, subordinators, and parallel structures</u>.

NOTE: You should use coordinators and subordinators only where you see brackets that tell you which logical relationship to show.

EXAMPLE: *[subordinator—contrast]*   The child is hungry.
The child is stubborn.
The child refuses to eat.

SOLUTION: Although the stubborn child is hungry, he refuses to eat.

For each set of sentences, create one sentence, joining related ideas with coordinators, subordinators, and parallel structures and modifying nouns with adjectives and prepositional phrases.

EXAMPLE: Plastics have been around for over a century.
[coordinator—effect]   We now take them for granted.

SOLUTION: Plastics have been around for over a century, so we now take them for granted.

1.   Our lifestyle depends heavily on plastics.
Our lifestyle is modern.
Our lifestyle is convenient.
[subordinator or coordinator—cause]   They are lightweight, resistant to corrosion, and durable.

2.   *[subordinator—condition]*   We look around.
We can see that this marvel has practically invaded our society.
The marvel is synthetic.

3.   Pans, windows, and bumpers are a few items that have made our lives easier.
The pans are non-stick.
The pans are Teflon-coated.
The windows are shatterproof.
The windows are plastic.
The bumpers are nonrusting.
The bumpers are plastic.
The bumpers are on cars.
[coordinator—contrast]   Plastics have also become a menace.
The menace is to our environment.

4. *[subordinator—cause]* Plastic does not decompose.
    Wastes accumulate in piles.
    The piles are enormous.
    The piles are unsanitary.
    The piles are in city dumps.

5. *[subordinator—cause]* Ocean dumping used to be legal.
    Our oceans are now filled with plastics.
    The plastics are dangerous.

6. Every year, trash kills or maims thousands.
    The trash is floating.
    The trash is plastic.
    The thousands are of sea creatures.

7. As many as 40,000 seals die from starvation or strangulation each year.
    [subordinator—time] They become entangled in netting and packing straps.
    The netting and packing straps are plastic.

8. Many sea creatures eat bags and fishing lines that resemble jellyfish or plankton.
    The bags and lines are plastic.
    [coordinator—effect] They die from stomach blockage or bleeding.
    The bleeding is internal.

9. The effects are devastating.
    The effects are of plastics disposal.
    [coordinator—contrast]   Some solutions may be on the horizon.

10. Some scientists can make products.
    The products are biodegradable.
    The products are plastic.
    The products are from a mixture.
    The mixture is of cornstarch and plastic.
    [subordinator—contrast]   Scientists worry that the dust could be harmful
    to breathe.
    The dust is fine.
    The dust is of plastic.
    The plastic is decomposing.

11. Other scientists think wastes could be burned for fuel.
    The wastes are plastic.
    [subordinator or coordinator—cause]   Most plastic is made from petroleum.

12. The idea seems good.
    The idea is of burning plastic for fuel.
    [subordinator—condition]   Technology for burning can be developed.
    The burning is safe.
    The burning is of plastic.

13. Meanwhile, the whales, seals, and turtles must wait for a generation to work
     out a solution.
     The generation is new.
     The generation is of scientists.
     The scientists are knowledgeable.
     The scientists are concerned.
     The solution is to our plastic waste problem.

In the following exercise, you will not be given any cues signaling when to use joining words, so this exercise may seem more challenging than previous review exercises. And although these exercises call for structures you have already worked with in this book, you may come up with alternative ways to combine some of these more open sentence sets.

EXAMPLE: Perhaps you have a pen or a bracelet.
The pen is lucky.
The pen is for writing "A" essays.
The bracelet is favorite.
The bracelet is of lucky charms.
You keep your superstitions secret.

SOLUTION: Perhaps you have a lucky pen for writing "A" essays or a favorite bracelet of lucky charms, but you keep your superstitions secret.

1. You may be embarrassed to admit to your superstitions.
People have had superstitions.
The people are from all cultures and times.
The superstitions are about events and objects.
The events are natural.

2a. The rabbit's foot was a symbol.
The symbol was of good luck.
The symbol was for Celtic tribes.
The Celtic tribes were in Western Europe around 600 B.C.
Celtic tribes believed the rabbit was in contact with forces.
The rabbit was burrowing.
The forces were mysterious.
The forces were from the underground.

2b. The rabbit bears young quite frequently.
The Celtic people considered the rabbit a symbol.
The symbol was powerful.
The symbol was of fertility.

2c. They came to treasure the rabbit's foot.
     They believed it could promote fertility.
     The fertility was in women.

3a. Adults knock on wood.
     The adults are boasting.
     They are participating in a 4,000-year-old ritual.
     The ritual is Native American Indian.

3b. The Native American Indians believed that boasting could bring bad luck.
     The boasting was about a future accomplishment.
     They sought to appease the gods by knocking on an oak tree.

4a. Many of us know about the tradition.
     The tradition is of breaking a wishbone.
     We may not know its origins.

4b. The Etruscans believed that hens and roosters were prophets.
     The Etruscans were ancient.
     The Etruscans were in Italy.
     The hens were squawking before laying an egg.
     The roosters were crowing to "foretell" a new day.

4c. Originally, the Etruscans made wishes by stroking the bones.
The bones were unbroken.
The bones were dried.
The bones were clavicle.
The bones were of roosters and hens.

4d. Later, the practice changed.
The practice was of stroking the clavicle.
The reason is not especially mysterious.
The reason is for this change.

4e. Eventually, the custom came about.
The custom was of two people.
The people were tugging at the wishbone to get the larger half.
Too many people wanted to make wishes on too few wishbones.

4f. This superstition survives today in our expression "to get a lucky break."
The superstition is of the wishbone.

5a. We all have heard that walking brings bad luck.
The walking is under a ladder.
Most are unaware that this superstition goes back to about 3,000 B.C. in Egypt.

5b. The triangle represented a trinity.
     The triangle was created when a ladder was leaned against a wall.
     The trinity was sacred.
     The trinity was of gods.

5c. People walked under a ladder.
     They would be violating space.
     The space was sacred.

6a. A new baby is born.
     The parents sometimes tell their children that the stork delivered the baby down
     the chimney.
     This explanation is confusing today.

6b. The Scandinavians originated the story.
     The Scandinavians were ancient.
     The story is of the stork.
     The Scandinavians admired the birds.
     The birds are long-lived.
     The birds are monogamous.

6c. The Scandinavians noticed that storks lavished attention on their parents.
     The storks were adult.
     The storks were nesting in chimney tops.
     Their parents were elderly.

6d. The stork, therefore, became a symbol.
     The symbol is of a life.
     The life is long.
     The life is happy.
     The life is domestic.

7.   Our society relies on explanations.
     Our society is "civilized."
     The explanations are scientific.
     Many people still count on superstitions.
     The superstitions are passed down from earlier generations.
     Many even create their own superstitious beliefs.

Unit Eleven

Modifying Nouns with Appositives

Among the words that can modify nouns are nouns themselves. For instance, we sometimes use noun modifiers next to (before or after) the nouns they describe.

> The cab driver opened the door for his passenger, <u>a tall *woman* in a strapless red dress</u>.

Woman is a noun that makes it clear to the reader who the passenger is; the word *woman* plus the modifiers *tall* and *in a strapless red dress* rename *passenger* in a specific way. We call the underlined descriptive phrase an <u>appositive</u>, which is a word or phrase containing a noun that renames the noun it modifies.

More Examples:

> My best friend, <u>a cat with a loud purr</u>, always knows how to cheer me up.

> She went to see Humphrey Bogart in a romantic movie, <u>the fifth one she'd seen in a week</u>.

> Marvin, <u>a straight A student in chemistry</u>, ignited his lab partner's hair with the bunson burner, <u>a device Marvin should never have touched</u>.

Punctuation with Appositives

Set off single modifying phrases with commas:

> Carlos met his girlfriend at the health club, <u>the local hangout</u>.

If the appositive comes in the middle of a sentence, enclose it in commas:

> Carlos met his girlfriend, <u>a disc jockey</u>, at the health club.

Set off a series of appositives with dashes:

> Carlos and his girlfriend enjoy similar things—<u>cartoons, Diet Coke, spandex leotards, and mirrors</u>.
> Their friends—<u>sun-tanned gods and goddesses, the state's best aerobic instructor, and the local DJ</u>—like to get together to party.

Or use a colon to set off a list of appositives at the end of a sentence:

> Bart wrote the following items on his shopping list: <u>Frostie Fritters Cereal, strawberry milk, hot dogs, canned dog food, and paper towels</u>.

Exercise One The Ski Trip

Combine the sentence pairs by eliminating, in the second sentence, the noun that repeats the noun in the first sentence. Also eliminate any forms of the verb *be* so that you reduce the second sentence to an appositive that modifies the underlined noun in the first sentence.

EXAMPLE: Most students cannot wait until <u>semester break</u>.
~~Semester break is~~ a time to relax and forget about deadlines and exams.

SOLUTION: Most students cannot wait until semester break, <u>a time to relax and forget about deadlines and exams</u>.

1. <u>Sammy</u> found herself bored on her winter break from school.
Sammy was a short, red-haired drama major.

2. So Sammy called her friend <u>Rhoda</u>.
Rhoda was a tall, brown-haired physics major.

3. Finally, Sammy and Rhoda decided to go on a ski <u>trip</u>.
The trip was a fun, fantastic, fantasy escape.

4. First, they made reservations at the <u>Big Bear Hut</u>.
The Hut was a ski lodge in Bear Valley.

5. Then, Sammy and Rhoda rented their <u>supplies</u>.
The supplies were skis by Rossignol and boots by Fischer.

6. But then the two friends took their most important <u>step</u>.
   The step was a trip to the mall for sexy ski wear.

7. Sammy found some gorgeous <u>clothes</u>.
   The clothes were emerald green stretch pants, a matching shirt, and a white vest.

8. Rhoda also found some sexy <u>separates</u>.
   The separates were light blue stretch pants, a navy blue turtleneck, and
   a multicolored vest.

9. Sammy and Rhoda packed their ski clothes and their best party <u>garb</u>.
   The garb was the kind that would lure any man their way.

Exercise Two   Not So Typical Music Listeners

Combine each group of sentences below by reducing the last two sentences in each group to appositives that modify nouns in the first sentence. Note that the nouns aren't underlined, so look to see what is being repeated and cross out repeated nouns and forms of the verb *be* before you do any sentence combining.

EXAMPLE: Most people enjoy music.
~~The people are~~ those of any age.
~~Music is~~ a kind of medicine for the soul.

SOLUTION: Most people, those of any age, enjoy music, a kind of medicine for the soul.

1.   Heavy metal is supposed to attract crowds of long-haired, maladjusted teens.
Heavy metal is music with loud electric guitars and drums.
The maladjusted teens are young people who rebel against their parents.

2.   But my Uncle Walter enjoys listening to heavy metal.
Uncle Walter is a 40-year-old, bald accountant.
His heavy metal is usually some song by Arrows and Petunias.

3.   On the other hand, modern rock is supposed to attract hordes of modern teenagers.
Modern rock is music featuring vocals and acoustics.
The teenagers are boys who are addicted to MTV and girls who dream of dating the lead singers.

4.   But my Aunt Wilma listens to modern rock.
Aunt Wilma is a 50-year-old housewife.
Modern rock is any new release by D-Fresch Load.

5. Soft rock is supposed to attract people like Walter and Wilma.
    Soft rock is background music often played in elevators.
    Walter and Wilma are people who wear polyester suits.

6. Yet Walter and Wilma's 13-year-old daughter loves listening to soft rock.
    Their daughter is Winnifred.
    Soft rock is any Barry Manilow song that plays in elevators or dentists' offices.

7. Rap music songs are supposed to attract only adolescents.
    The songs are usually popular ballads that need no instruments.
    The adolescents are those with asymmetrical Barnie Brown haircuts.

8. However, Walter's mother really gets into rap.
    Walter's mother is a 75-year-old woman with arthritis.
    Rap is her excuse to limber up her joints and idolize Lazy B.

Creating Appositives

Writers can use noun phrase appositives effectively to give readers helpful, specific information and to condense their many ideas in a logical and sophisticated way. In the previous exercises, you practiced combining sentences; in the following exercise, you will create some of your own appositives. The nouns to be modified are underlined, and blanks are provided so that you can add specific information with appositives.

> EXAMPLE: Too many people today need to find a suitable <u>companion</u>,
>
> _____
>
> SOLUTION: Too many people today need to find a suitable companion, <u>a dog who loves them unconditionally, a cat who keeps them warm at night, a guinea pig who never complains about the cooking, or a spouse with a large bank account</u>.

Exercise Three   Alfred and Edward

1. My friend Alfred spends his afternoons watching his favorite <u>program</u> on "Trash T.V.,"

    _____

2. On the other hand, my cousin Edward spends his afternoons at his favorite <u>video stores</u> in the mall—

    _____

    _____

3. Finally bored with their usual pastimes, Alfred and Edward met me last Friday at my favorite <u>club</u>,

    _____

4. <u>Alfred and Edward</u>, two _____, danced the night away with some lovely women and they learned some of the following <u>songs</u>:

    _____

    _____

5. But the next day, Alfred went back to his old <u>habit</u>, _____, and Edward went back to the local <u>mall</u>,

    _____

Exercise Four   Madge and Mordred
_____

What follows is a hypothetical love story, one that features the meeting and eventual marriage of Madge and Mordred. You are to fill in the blanks with noun phrase modifiers (appositives). If you have any difficulty coming up with appositives, try asking yourself some questions about the underlined nouns.

Madge, (1) _____, was

a newly divorced woman. So she decided to try a computer dating service and called

her friend Mary Frances, (2) _____,

someone who had signed up with many agencies in the past. Mary Frances told Madge

to contact the Best Bet Dating Spa, (3) _____.

Mary Frances promised Madge that she was sure to meet with success. On Saturday

morning, Madge left her apartment, (4) _____,

and set out for the Best Bet Spa. The spa, on the corner of Fifth Street and Vine,

looked like an impressive structure, (5) _____.

Inside, Madge met the director, Mr. Rogers, (6) _____,

someone she felt very comfortable talking to. After she filled out the

application, she went home and waited. Later that week, Madge's phone,

(7) _____, rang. A young

man named Mordred was on the line and said, in a voice that grabbed Madge

immediately, that he had gotten her number from Best Bet. Mordred said he knew

they were meant for each other when he heard that they like the same kinds of music—

(8) _____. Mordred also

suggested that they go on a date the next week, and Madge readily accepted, agreeing to meet him on Friday night at Woof, Purr, Whistle and Thump, his

favorite <u>hangout</u>, (9) _____. When they met, Madge first

noticed Mordred's <u>eyes</u>, (10) _____,

and Mordred fell in love with Madge's <u>feet</u>, (11) _____.

Actually, it was love at first sight for both. Married now for three years, Madge and

Mordred share their <u>dreams</u>, (12) _____.

Exercise Five   You Be the Author

1.   Write a sentence in which you use an appositive to describe a movie or a singing group you enjoy.

2.   Write a sentence in which you use an appositive to describe a car you would enjoy driving.

3.   Write a sentence in which you use an appositive to describe your best friend.

4.   Write a sentence in which you use an appositive to describe your favorite form of entertainment.

5.   Write a sentence in which you use an appositive to describe your favorite place.

   Next, write five sentences about the topic you're currently writing about in your writing class, and try to use appositives to describe some of the nouns in your sentences.

6.

7.

8.

9.

10.

Join the sentences below by adding noun modifiers (adjectives, prepositional phrases, and appositives) to the base sentences and by joining sentences using coordinators, subordinators, and parallel structures. The nouns to be modified are underlined, and joining techniques are given in brackets. Cross out any repeated words and forms of *be* in the sentences containing modifiers.

> EXAMPLE: Most of us think about our <u>future</u>.
> ~~The future is~~ the next hour.
> ~~The future is~~ the next day.
> ~~The future is~~ the next week.
> *[coordinator—contrast]*   The future may be years from now.

> SOLUTION: Most of us think about our future—the next hour, the next day, or the next week—but the future may be years from now.

1. *[subordinator—time]*   We think about the future.
    We are forced to make <u>decisions</u>.
    The decisions are about our education, career, and family.
    The decisions are based on our motivation.
    The decisions are based on our attitude toward risk-taking.
    The decisions are based on our sense of obligation.

2. Some <u>people</u> need to make plans for the rest of their lives.
    These people are future-oriented.
    These people are the ones who make daily lists of their goals.
    [subordinator—contrast]   Other <u>people</u> live each day as if it were their last.
    These people are present-oriented.
    These people are the ones who live for the moment.

3. All research studies agree that our "time sense" can greatly affect our lives.
    [coordinator—contrast]   Some studies have shown that attitudes toward the future differ according to age, sex, income, and occupation.

4. According to a study done by Alexander Gonzales, most <u>adults</u> are more concerned about the future than teenagers are.
    The adults are those 40 years old or older.
    [coordinator—effect]   This future planning is a tendency that increases with age.

5. In addition, the study claims that middle-aged <u>men</u> are more likely to plan for the future than middle-aged <u>women</u> are.
    The men are generally fathers and professionals responsible for their families' financial security.
    The women are usually housewives and mothers who have achieved their goals.
    [coordinator—contrast]   Perhaps these attitudes will change as women and men change their expectations.
    The expectations are of their roles in society.

6. People who earn poor <u>salaries</u> worry mainly about the present.
    The salaries are incomes less than $16,000 per year.
    [coordinator—contrast]   They may tend to be fatalistic individuals.
    The individuals are people who believe that for them, no future exists.

7. <u>People</u> tend to fall into both <u>camps</u>.
    The people are with higher incomes.
    The camps are those who live for the moment.
    The camps are those who make goals and subgoals.
    [coordinator—cause]   These people can afford to make choices.

8. Finally, according to the study, most people tend to pick certain occupations for themselves.
    [subordinator—cause]   They may already have the time sense needed for the chosen occupation.

Unit Twelve

Modifying Nouns with Adjective Clauses

In this unit, you will again be working with structures that modify nouns—adjective clauses. Like appositives, adjective clauses are a good way to add descriptive details to nouns. The following sentences contain adjective clauses:

> The student <u>who aced his exam</u> was happy.
> The exam, <u>which covered six chapters of trigonometry</u>, determined the final course grade.

We call the underlined structures "adjective clauses" because, like simple adjectives, they describe nouns. In the above sentences, the adjective clause *who aced his exam* describes *student*, and the adjective clause *which covered six chapters of trigonometry* describes *exam*.

We call the underlined structures "clauses" because they are made up of a subject—*who, that,* or *which*—and a verb. But they are dependent clauses, so they cannot be sentences by themselves. And like other modifiers of more than one word, they come after the nouns they modify.

In the exercises in this unit, you will be joining two sentences by making the second one into an adjective clause. Follow these steps:

1. Find the word in the second sentence that either repeats or refers to the underlined noun in the first sentence.
2. Cross out the word that you found and change it to *who, that,* or *which.*
3. Change the second sentence into an adjective clause and place it in the first sentence after the noun it modifies.

The following are examples and explanations for the combined sentences using adjective clauses.

EXAMPLE A:	<u>Mary</u> is a volunteer English teacher in the Marshall Islands. who ~~Mary~~ grew up in California.
SOLUTION:	Mary, <u>who grew up in California</u>, is a volunteer teacher in the Marshall Islands.
EXPLANATION:	*Mary* is repeated in the second sentence and is a person word, so *Mary* can be replaced with *who.*
EXAMPLE B:	<u>The students</u> study their core subjects in English. who ~~They~~ usually spend most of their lives on the islands.
SOLUTION:	The students, <u>who spend most of their lives on the islands</u>, study their core subjects in English.

EXPLANATION: *They* in the second sentence refers back to *students* in the first sentence. Here *they* refers to people, so *they* can be replaced with *who*.

EXAMPLE C: Many volunteers live with island families in thatched-roof <u>huts</u>. that ~~The huts~~ don't have electricity or running water.

SOLUTION: Many volunteers live with island families in thatched-roof huts <u>that don't have electricity or running water</u>.

EXPLANATION: *Huts* is repeated in the second sentence, and *huts* are things, so *huts* can be replaced with *that*.

EXAMPLE D: <u>The Marshall Islands</u> are located in the central Pacific Ocean. which ~~They~~ consist of five islands and 29 atolls.

SOLUTION: The Marshall Islands, <u>which consist of five islands and 29 atolls</u>, are located in the central Pacific Ocean.

EXPLANATION: *They* in the second sentence refers back to *Marshall Islands* in the first sentence, and *islands* are things, so *they* can be replaced by *which*.

EXAMPLE E: The land <u>area</u> is only 70 square miles. Coconut trees dominate ~~it~~. which

SOLUTION: The land area, <u>which coconut trees dominate</u>, is only 70 square miles.

EXPLANATION: *It* in the second sentence refers to *area* in the first sentence. Since *it* is a thing, we can replace *it* with *which*. We change the word order in the adjective clause so that *which* follows the noun it modifies.

Exercise One   Nirvana and the Law

In each of the sentence pairs below, a noun or pronoun in the second sentence either repeats or refers to a noun in the first sentence. Change the noun in the second sentence to *who*, *which*, or *that* so that the second sentence can become an adjective clause modifying a noun in the first sentence.

EXAMPLE: My good friend <u>Colleen</u> likes to engage in illegal activity.
            <u>She</u> claims to be a daredevil by nature.

SOLUTION: My good friend Colleen, <u>who claims to be a daredevil by nature</u>, likes to engage in illegal activity.

1.   The illegal <u>activity</u> may require that Colleen show her I.D.
      <u>It</u> involves her red Triumph Spitfire.

2.   Often, Colleen must try to avoid the <u>police</u>.
      <u>They</u> try to catch her.

3.   To get away with her scheme, Colleen must thoroughly plan a <u>course</u>.
      <u>It</u> covers half the city.

4.   She must also follow her plan carefully to get to her <u>destination</u>.
      She will reach <u>it</u> without getting caught if she is lucky.

5.   To add to her daring <u>feat</u>, Colleen dons a tight black body suit and matching goggles.
      The <u>feat</u> calls for the appropriate clothing.

6. She also wears a red <u>scarf</u> around her neck.
    The <u>scarf</u> matches her Spitfire.

7. As Colleen covers her route, she listens to loud <u>music</u>.
    The <u>music</u> reaches deep within her psyche.

8. During her excursion, <u>Colleen</u> reaches an altered state.
    <u>Colleen</u> needs no drugs.

9. Yet through it all, she remains alert enough to watch out for <u>others</u>.
    The <u>others</u> are going slower than the speed limit.

Exercise Two   The Lonesome Cowboy

In the last exercise with sentence pairs, you reduced some sentences to adjective clauses by looking for repeated nouns or pronoun referents like *she* or *it* that could be replaced with *who*, *which*, or *that*, and then you modified nouns with your new adjective clauses. The following exercise is similar, but it introduces another common signal for reducing some sentences to adjective clauses.

EXAMPLE: Many people romanticize American cowboys.
            These cowboys rode the cattle trails after the Civil War.

SOLUTION: Many people romanticize American cowboys who rode the
             cattle trails after the Civil War.

EXPLANATION: We have turned the second sentence into an adjective clause
                modifying *cowboys* in the first sentence. The signal here is
                the word *these* + a repeated noun. Also watch for the signals
                this, that, and *those*.

1.   Cowboys actually were overworked and underpaid.
      These cowboys rode endless miles in rough weather.

2.   Cowboys rarely got enough sleep.
      Those cowboys worked 18 hours a day, every day of the week.

3.   Cowboys ate a boring daily diet.
      This diet usually consisted of beans, bacon, cornbread, and coffee.

4.   Cowboys often sang songs around campfires.
      Those songs revealed their loneliness and hard lives.

5. But cowboys rarely complained.
   Those cowboys had a lot to complain about.

6. Each cowboy found a way to entertain himself.
   This cowboy couldn't have a normal family life.

7. Some cowboys bought magazines.
   Cowboys read and passed along these magazines.

8. A cowboy's prize possession was his hat.
   He wore that hat during meals and sometimes to bed.

9. Cowboys also valued their boots.
   These boots often cost two months' wages.

10. People still commonly believe that cowboys were heroes.
    These heroes stand for the freedom of the Wild West.

Special Rule: Who/Whom

So far, you have used adjective clauses that begin with *who, that,* or *which*. Although you may need to refer to the previous section for some of the following exercises, this section will primarily clarify the difference between *who* and *whom*. Although both *who* and *whom* begin adjective clauses that modify person nouns, each has a separate grammatical function in the adjective clause it begins.

Take, for example, the following sentences containing adjective clauses:

My brother, [*who* married a crazy woman], has one crazy baby.
My sister-in-law, [*whom* my mother dislikes], is a fanatic.

Why do we use *who* in one adjective clause and *whom* in the other?
If we take the adjective clauses and turn them into sentences by replacing *who* or *whom* with a personal pronoun, we have the answer:

ADJECTIVE CLAUSE:

(my brother)	(my sister-in-law)
<u>who</u> married a crazy woman	<u>whom</u> my mother dislikes

SENTENCE:

<u>He</u> married a crazy woman.   My mother dislikes <u>her</u>.

EXPLANATION: The pronoun you placed in your sentence signals you to use

WHO for subject pronouns:	**WHOM** for object pronouns:
HE	HIM
SHE	HER
WE	US
THEY	THEM

REVIEW: To decide whether to use *who* or *whom*, follow these steps:

1. Identify and underline the words that make up the adjective clause.
2. Turn the adjective clause into a sentence by replacing *who* or *whom* with a personal pronoun from the previous list.
3. If you use a subject pronoun, use *who*, but if you use an object pronoun, use *whom*.

EXAMPLE: 1.   Our postman, <u>who/whom is usually prompt</u>, arrived late.
              2.   He is usually prompt.
              3.   He = *who*.

Exercise Three   Belinda and Sedrick

Follow the steps in the previous example and circle your choice of *who* or *whom*. In the first four sentences, Step 2 is done for you.

1. Belinda, (who/whom) shaved her head, volunteered to model for her art class. (She shaved her head.)

2. Sedrick, (who/whom) Belinda secretly adored, was a student in the same class. (Belinda secretly adored him.)

3. When she entered the room, Belinda, (who/whom) sported butcher knives as earrings, turned all eyes but Sedrick's. (She sported butcher knives as earrings.)

4. Sedrick, (who/whom) Belinda had asked out, had decided to play hard to get. (Belinda had asked him out.)

5. While the rest of the class sketched Belinda, Sedrick, (who/whom) was sketching a skull, flirted with the girl next to him.

6. Suddenly, Belinda, (who/whom) wished Sedrick would notice her, broke into tears.

7. So Sedrick raised his hand and complained about Belinda, (who/whom) he wanted to embarrass.

8. The instructor, (who/whom) wanted to embarrass Sedrick, forced Sedrick to join Belinda in front of the class.

9. As their classmates sketched and giggled, Belinda and Sedrick, (who/whom) by now felt ridiculous, were asked to arm wrestle.

10. Sedrick, (who/whom) Belinda beat in arm wrestling, took Belinda out to lunch after class.

Exercise Four   Blind Date

In this exercise, note what noun or pronoun in the second sentence either repeats or refers to a noun in the first sentence. Then turn the second sentence into an adjective clause beginning with *who* or *whom* and use it to modify the noun in the first sentence.

> EXAMPLE: Baxter had no plans for celebrating his 21st birthday.
> He had a tall, muscular body and dark curly hair.

> SOLUTION: Baxter, who had a tall muscular body and dark curly hair, had no plans for celebrating his 21st birthday.

1.   So Baxter decided to let his best friend Max fix him up with a blind date.
     Max had a taste for long-legged, romantic women.

2.   Max spent a great deal of time calling 976 "party line" numbers.
     Bax had known him for 15 years.

3.   While talking on the line about a week before, Max had spoken with a young woman.
     He thought she would be the ideal date for Baxter.

4.   The woman said that she would be happy to meet Baxter.
     The woman referred to herself as Cinderella.
     The woman called him her Prince Charming.

5.   So Max arranged for Bax to meet Cinderella the following Wednesday.
     Bax was incredibly nervous.

6. Max drove <u>Bax</u> to the meeting place, a local Denny's.
   <u>Bax</u> did not have a car.

7. Max literally had to shove <u>Bax</u> into the restaurant.
   Three 75-year-old ladies roaming around the parking lot pinched <u>Bax</u>.

8. <u>Bax</u> finally sat down on the yellow vinyl couch near the door.
   <u>Bax</u> had been twisting his burgundy bow tie for hours.

9. Baxter grew impatient after watching nine single <u>women</u> walk in.
   The <u>women</u> caused his heart to palpitate.

10. Finally, his <u>Cinderella</u> wiggled through the door.
    <u>Cinderella</u> sent his senses roaring with her purple leather mini-dress.

Exercise Five   Rio

Like appositives, adjective clauses enable writers to effectively join their ideas and show their readers what they mean. So it makes sense not only to practice joining ideas using adjective clauses, but also to create adjective clause modifiers.

Below is a hypothetical mystery story in which there are nouns that could be made more specific with adjective clauses, although you might also want to use a few appositives. The nouns to be modified are underlined, and blanks for your modifiers are provided.

One day, Matilda sat in a cafe, sipping cappuccino and talking with her friend

Jacquita, (1) _____. Matilda was telling

Jacquita about her husband Merv, (2) _____.

Apparently, Merv had turned into a very mysterious man, (3) _____

_____, and Matilda suspected that he was now involved in some criminal activity

(4) _____. Recently, Merv brought home some very disgusting

friends (5) _____. And he purchased

three expensive new cars, (6) _____.

But when Matilda, (7) _____,

questioned Merv about his activities, he ran out the front door. Despondent,

Matilda knew that her best friend Jacquita would know how to solve the problem,

(8) _____.

Jacquita recommended that Matilda do one of two things: hire a private detective to

find out what Merv had gotten himself into or sell the cars and run away to Rio. Matilda

decided to hire a detective (9) _____.

So the next day, the detective she'd hired followed Merv to work and to his favorite hangout, (10) _____. But

unfortunately, the detective lost Merv when Merv entered a K-Mart. When the

detective tried to call Matilda to let her know what had happened, a policewoman,

(11) _____, answered the phone.

The policewoman informed the detective that Matilda (12) _____

_____, had been arrested at the airport for possession of a stolen

car, (13) _____, and that Jacquita was last seen

boarding a plane, holding a cup of cappuccino in one hand and an airline ticket to Rio in

the other.

Exercise Six   You Be the Author

1.   Write a sentence in which you use an adjective clause to describe a person you know.

2.   Write a sentence in which you use an adjective clause to describe your home.

3.   Write a sentence in which you use an adjective clause to describe a home you'd like to own.

4.   Write a sentence in which you use an adjective clause to describe a book you've read. (The noun you describe can be the title of the book.)

5.   Write a sentence in which you use an adjective clause to describe a place you often visit.

Next, write five sentences about the topic you're currently writing about in your writing class. Try to use adjective clauses to describe the people, things, or ideas you're writing about.

6.

7.

8.

9.

10.

Unit Thirteen

Modifying Sentences with Verbal Phrases

Although verbs in sentences tell the time, or tense, verbals do not; they have other functions in sentences. Three verbal forms—the *-ing* form, or present participle; the *-ed* form, or past participle; and the *to* form, or infinitive—can be used to form verbal phrases. (See Unit One for a review of present and past participle verb forms.) In the following examples, you can see how the verbal phrases come from verbs:

EXAMPLE 1: Jamari was hoping to attract Jeff's attention.
Jamari honked her horn loudly.

SOLUTION: <u>Hoping to attract Jeff's attention</u>, Jamari honked her horn loudly.
or Jamari honked her horn loudly, <u>hoping to attract Jeff's attention</u>.

EXAMPLE 2: Jeff was frightened by the frantic honking.
He got off the freeway at the first exit.

SOLUTION: <u>Frightened by the frantic honking</u>, Jeff got off the freeway at the first exit. or Jeff got off the freeway at the first exit, <u>frightened by the frantic honking</u>.

EXAMPLE 3: Jamari wanted to find Jeff.
She got off at the next exit and doubled back.

SOLUTION: <u>To find Jeff</u>, Jamari got off at the next exit and doubled back.
or Jamari got off at the next exit and doubled back <u>to find Jeff</u>.

Verbal phrases are good ways to show that two actions happened at the same time:

1. *hoping + honked*
2. *frustrated + got off*
3. *to find + got off*

But often verbal phrases also show the <u>purpose</u> for an action in the sentence:

1. *Jamari honked her horn. Why? because she was hoping to attract Jeff's attention.*
2. *Jeff got off the freeway. Why? because he was frustrated by the heavy traffic.*
3. *Jamari got off at the next exit. Why? because she wanted to find Jeff.*

So verbal phrases have two functions:

1. To show a time relationship between the action in the verbal phrase and the action in the main clause of the sentence.
2. To show the purpose of the action in the main clause.

When you use verbal phrases, you have to follow one important rule: The doer of the action in the verbal phrase has to be a noun or pronoun in the main clause of the sentence, usually the sentence subject.

In sentence 1, who was hoping to attract Jeff's attention? _____

Who honked her horn? _____

Notice that the following sentence does not make sense:

incorrect: Reaching out her right arm, the ball was dunked into the basket.

The verbal phrase does not make sense with the subject of the sentence because the noun *ball* cannot do the action *reaching*. To correct this sentence, make the sentence subject be a noun that can do the action in the verbal phrase:

correct: Reaching out her right arm, the player dunked the ball into the basket.

Exercise One   Going Out to Eat

Join the sets of sentences below, making the second sentence into a verbal phrase. You may place the verbal phrase before or after the main sentence; you will have to decide whether or not the verbal phrase can make sense in either position. (Sometimes the verbal phrase will only make sense in one of these positions.)

EXAMPLE: Rita read the latest restaurant reviews.
She wanted to find a good restaurant.

SOLUTION: <u>To find a good restaurant</u>, Rita read the latest restaurant reviews.
or Rita read the latest restaurant reviews <u>to find a good restaurant</u>.

1.   Jamal and Rita studied the "Yellow Pages" all Saturday afternoon.
They were <u>looking</u> for a good restaurant that would please Rita's parents.

2.   Jamal offered to help pay for the dinner.
He was <u>hoping</u> Rita would go for a steak house.

3.   Rita refused his offer.
She was <u>accustomed</u> to paying her own way.

4.   She also vetoed the steak house idea.
She was <u>concerned</u> that her vegetarian mother would feel left out at a steak house.

5.   Jamal suggested a vegetarian diner called "The Lean Bean."
He wanted <u>to simplify</u> the problem.

6. But Rita rejected this suggestion also.
    She was <u>exclaiming</u> that "The Lean Bean" served tasteless alfalfa hot dogs and
    rubbery soybean "chicken."

7. She said they should find a restaurant that also served meat.
    She was <u>thinking</u> of her carnivorous dad.

8. Jamal and Rita began to bicker.
    They were <u>frustrated</u> at their failure to find a satisfactory restaurant.

9. Jamal finally noticed the name, in tiny print, of a Middle Eastern restaurant.
    He was desperately <u>seeking</u> a place that would please everyone.

10. Rita phoned "Ali's Place" for their list of dinner entrees.
    She wanted <u>to be</u> on the safe side.

11. The restaurant served juicy skewered lamb for Rita's father and spicy meatless falafel
    for her mother.
    It was <u>offering</u> a diverse assortment of entrees.

12. Jamal and Rita left the restaurant smiling that night.
    They were <u>satisfied</u> with their selection.

Exercise Two   The Economics Final

Verbal phrases can often be good alternatives to subordinate clauses that show cause/effect or time relationships. In this exercise, you'll revise the sentences by making the underlined subordinate clauses into verbal phrases. Notice that the subject of each subordinate clause beginning with *because* and *since* or *before*, *after* and *while* is also the subject of the main clause; that's your clue that you can make the subordinate clause into a verbal phrase.

EXAMPLE: <u>Because she wanted to help the students do well on the final exam</u>, the economics teacher reviewed the lectures in class.

SOLUTION: **(In order) to help the students do well on the final exam**, the economics teacher reviewed the lectures in class.

EXAMPLE: <u>After she reviewed the lectures</u>, the economics teacher gave the students a practice test.

SOLUTION: **After reviewing the lectures**, the economics teacher gave the students a practice test.

1.   <u>Because she was determined to get an A on the final</u>, Maria studied every night.

2.   <u>Since he hoped to get at least a C</u>, Norman crammed the night before the test.

3.   <u>Before she quizzed herself</u>, Maria reviewed each chapter of the textbook.

4.   <u>Because she guessed that the final would be like the practice test</u>, Maria looked up the answers she missed on the test.

5. <u>Before he settled down to study,</u>
   Norman ate dinner and watched a movie.

6. <u>While she was studying,</u>
   Maria took a break every hour.

7. <u>After he finished the final exam,</u>
   Norman felt confident that he got at least a C.

8. <u>Because she knew all of the answers,</u>
   Maria felt confident that she got an A.

9. <u>After she saw how well her students did on the final,</u>
   the teacher gave the class a day off.

10. <u>Since they wanted to celebrate,</u>
    the students spent a day at the beach.

Creating Verbal Phrases

Exercise Three   Fitness Folly

Create your own *-ing*, past participle and infinitive verbal phrases to complete the sentences below. Remember that a noun in the main clause must be able to do the action in the verbal phrase. Most likely, you will have an easier time coming up with *-ing* phrases, but try to come up with the two other forms as well.

> EXAMPLE: _____, Ethel decided she should get in shape.

> SOLUTION: Looking in the mirror, Ethel decided she should get in shape.

1. _____, Ethel wanted to find an exercise plan she could stick to.

2. She tried aerobics, _____.

3. But poor Ethel, _____, embarrassed herself in front of the whole class.

4. _____, she gave up on aerobics and turned to ballet.

5. _____, she had to give up on ballet too.

6. _____, Ethel began lessons at the local swimming pool, _____.

7. _____, Ethel discovered she was allergic to chlorine!

8. Ethel, _____, decided to take up a martial art.

9. She was a success at this activity, so she's been practicing it ever since,

_____

Unit Fourteen

Final Review Exercises

In all of the following exercises, you will use all of the modifiers and joining techniques you have practiced in the book. Your goal is to make each set of sentences into one sentence.

1. In the late 18th and early 19th centuries, St. Louis, Missouri, played a significant role.
   The role was in westward expansion.

2. Ordinary people were drawn to the western reaches of the United States.
   The people hoped for a better place to work and raise children.

3. St. Louis was a source for western commercial ventures.
   St. Louis was a starting point for pioneer journeys west.

4. Steamboats lined the Mississippi River levee.
   The levee was cluttered with cargo.

5. The streets were filled with shops.
   The shops were blacksmith shops, gun shops, general stores, and taverns.

6. In 1934, a group of St. Louis citizens formed the Jefferson National Expansion Memorial Association.
   The citizens wanted to establish a memorial.

7.   The memorial would honor Thomas Jefferson.
     The memorial would honor people.
     The people left their eastern and midwestern homes.
     The people wanted to travel to the unknown western frontier.

8.   The citizens' group chose the city's riverfront areas as the site for the memorial.
     The riverfront area was the original location of the city.

9.   The riverfront memorial park has a central feature.
     The central feature is a 630-foot arch.
     The arch is stainless steel.
     The arch was designed by Eero Saarinen.
     Saarinen was an architect.

10. The memorial honors homesteaders.
     The homesteaders had crops.
     The crops were devastated by weather.
     The crops were devastated by plagues.
     The plagues were of grasshoppers.

11. The St. Louis Gateway Arch memorializes struggles.
     The St. Louis Gateway Arch memorializes defeats.
     The St. Louis Gateway Arch memorializes triumphs.

1. Today most cars have license plates.
    The plates are numbered.
    The plates are registered in a particular state.
    A century ago most vehicles had no identification.

2. According to an old legend, an incident spurred the invention.
    The incident was peculiar.
    The incident was involving a buggy driver and a policeman.
    The invention was of the license tag.

3. Apparently, the buggy driver was speeding through town.
    He was driving recklessly and scaring old ladies.
    A policeman stopped him.

4. The policeman could not issue the driver a ticket.
    The policeman wanted to keep his streets safe.
    A ticket was for speeding.
    He demanded that the driver appear in court the next day.
    The driver was to be charged with disturbing the peace.

5. The policeman learned the man's name and his address.
    The name was "Egbert Main."
    The policeman discovered that the man had lied.
    The man didn't show up in court the next day.
    The man gave an address.
    The address would have been in the middle of the river.
    The river was the Hudson.

6.   After several similar incidents and the invention, the New York Legislature passed
     the first law.
     The incidents were involving dishonest drivers.
     The invention was of the automobile.
     The law was requiring auto owners to register their cars.

7.   All auto owners would receive a tag.
     The owners paid $1 to register.
     The tag was aluminum.
     The tag was about the size of a half-dollar.
     The tag was stamped with a number and "New York State."
     Individual auto owners could choose how to display their tag.

8.   New York's system was soon copied.
     The system was of keeping track of the new motor cars.
     The system was soon copied by other states and other countries.
     Each state or country had its own style.
     The style was of license tags.

9.   In the United States, for instance, the license plate has a history.
     The history is of different sizes, shapes, colors, and slogans.
     Each state picks its tag's colors.
     The colors are changed almost every year.

10. On one of its plates, Arizona once used copper.
    The copper was to promote the state's most important metal.
    Illinois once used tags.
    The tags were of pressed fiber and soybeans.
    The tags were to preserve steel.
    Steel was scarce during World War II.

11. The soybean tags looked fine.
    They didn't last long.
    Dogs and cows ate them.

12. All states have agreed on the same size.
    The size is for the plate.
    The size is 6 by 12 inches.
    Most states have retained their own slogans and symbols.
    The slogans and the symbols are for the license plates.
    The slogans are sayings like "America's Dairyland," "Water Wonderland,"
    "Sportsman's Paradise," and "The Beef State."
    The symbols are drawings like bears, bells, and grapefruits.

13. The variety of license plates provides children some form of entertainment.
    The license plates are seen on highways.
    The children are bored on their long summer vacations.
    The children irritate their parents with their questions.
    The entertainment can teach them about specific industries or lifestyles in
    faraway states.

14. But by far, the most interesting, humorous, and often embarrassing plates are the personalized ones.
    They are the ones that reveal something about the driver.
    There is "CAKES" for a baker.
    There is "ROCK" and "ROLL" for two teenaged friends.
    There is "SEXYSR" for one dirty old man.
    There is even "IMEZRU" for one dirty young man.

1. Dreaming is a collection.
    The collection is of mental images.
    The mental images are fusions.
    The fusions are of pieces.
    The pieces are of memory and knowledge.
    The pieces arise during rapid eye movement (REM) sleep.

2. Humans experience REM sleep.
    Other mammals experience REM sleep.
    Birds experience REM sleep.
    REM sleep is characterized by movements, limbs, respiration, and heartbeat.
    The movements are rapid.
    The movements are of the eye.
    The limbs are immoblized.
    The respiration and heartbeat are irregular.

3. The act is part.
    The act is of dreaming.
    The part is of heritage.
    The heritage is human.
    The heritage is evolutionary.
    The heritage can be traced back 135 million years.

4. Some people believe dreams are phenomena.
    The phenomena are meaningless.
    Others believe that dreams may give us insight.
    The insight is greater than reality.
    Dreams bring together experiences with events.
    The experiences are current.
    The events are from our past.

5. Dreams are common. Dreams are of flying.
    Dreams are of walking naked in public.
    These experiences capture fears.
    These experiences capture hopes.
    The fears and hopes are human.
    Dreams vary depending on the age and sex.
    The age and sex are of the dreamer.

6. In the past, dreams differed.
    The dreams are of women and men.
    The women and men are American.

7. In the past, women dreamt of scenes.
    They dreamt of conversations.
    They dreamt of themselves as victims.
    The scenes were domestic.
    The conversations were emotional.
    They were victims of aggression.
    Men dreamt of the outdoors.
    Men dreamt of themselves as aggressors.

8. Now men and women have similar dreams.
    The dreams are of the outdoors.
    The dreams are of sex.
    The dreams are of themselves as aggressors.

9. The dreams have little content.
   The dreams are of children.
   The children are aged 3 to 5.
   The content is emotional.
   These children make appearances.
   The appearances are rare.
   The appearances are in their dreams.

10. Children dream in stories.
    The children are aged 5 and 6.
    The stories are of action.
    The dreamers are still not actors.
    The actors are in their own dreams.

11. By the age of 7 or 8, children dream like adults do.
    Children put themselves in their dreams.

12. Dreams are the most powerful.
    The dreams solve a problem.
    Many dreams represent a conflict.
    The conflict is unresolved.

13. Some psychologists believe we can control our dreams.
     We choose a problem before we go to sleep.
     We write about it before we go to sleep.
     We ask ourselves a question before we go to sleep.
     The problem is bothering us.
     The question is about the problem.

14. But we will forget our dreams.
     We will miss a possible answer.
     The answer is to our question.
     We don't write our dreams down.
     Dreams vanish within 15 minutes.

1.   Earthquakes are occurrences as old as mankind.
     Most ancients did not understand their cause.
     The ancients thought the earthquakes were acts of God.

2.   For instance, philosophers blamed earthquakes on Poseidon.
     The philosophers were ancient.
     Poseidon was the god of the sea.
     Tribes in Bulgaria believed that earthquakes struck when a water buffalo shifted
     its weight.
     The water buffalo was enormous.
     It shifted its weight to ease its discomfort.

3.   Early humans saw earthquakes as similar to other misfortunes.
     The misfortunes were natural.
     The misfortunes were caused by God.
     These early humans did not make additional attempts.
     The attempts were to understand earthquakes.

4.   But people in the 17th century became more interested in knowledge.
     The knowledge was scientific.
     They made attempts.
     The attempts were to record earthquakes.

5.   The earthquake occurred in Lisbon, Portugal.
     The earthquake was the first recorded.

6.   Records were kept by priests.
     The records were of deaths caused by earthquakes.
     The priests made the first attempt.
     The attempt was real.
     The attempt was to investigate earthquakes and their effects.

7.   Earthquakes are still not completely understood today.
     Geologists have agreed upon theories.
     The theories are based upon evidence.
     The evidence suggests that tremors result from the rebalancing.
     The rebalancing is of forces.
     The forces are arising from the collision.
     The collision is of plates.
     The plates are moving.
     The plates are of layered rock.
     The plates are floating upon the earth's interior.
     The interior is molten.

8.   Geologists think that over 200 million years ago there was one continental mass.
     The continental mass was one huge plate.
     The plate was of rock.
     Today that rock may have broken into 20 plates.
     The plates are sliding and colliding.

9. Some of the plates collide, usually at the intersection of continents and oceans.
The collision changes the geography.
The geography is of the earth.
The collision builds island foundations.
The collision makes mountains rise.
The collision elevates or lowers existing land masses.
The collision forces volcanoes to erupt.
The collision stimulates earthquakes.

10. Molten material from the earth's interior makes rifts.
The rifts are in the plates.
The plates are the newest.
The plates are beneath the ocean floor.
Then this process pushes plates slowly apart.
This process is called "sea spreading."

11. The plates move.
Their movement is causing friction.

12. Sometimes the plates lock together.
Their locking causes strain underneath them.
Their locking requires that the strain be relieved.
Rifts occur in new places or movement occurs within existing rifts.
The movement causes an earthquake.

13. Some plates move in a vertical direction.
The direction is up and down.
Other plates move in a lateral direction.
The direction is side to side.

14. The direction of the movement and several other factors contribute to the amount of destruction.
     The destruction is caused by the earthquake.
     One factor is the depth of the collision.
     Another factor is the interference that exists between the collision site and the epicenter of the quake.
     The interference is of rock, mountain, water, and flat land.

15. Earthquakes occur infrequently.
     The earthquakes are of large magnitude.
     The plates beneath our surface move regularly.
     The plates creep.
     The plates do not lock.